Making experience pay

Making experience pay
Management success through effective learning

Alan Mumford

McGRAW-HILL Book Company (UK) Limited

London · New York · St Louis · San Francisco · Auckland · Bogotá
Guatemala · Hamburg · Johannesburg · Lisbon · Madrid · Mexico
Montreal · New Delhi · Panama · Paris · San Juan · São Paulo
Singapore · Sydney · Tokyo · Toronto

Published by
McGRAW-HILL Book Company (UK) Limited
MAIDENHEAD · BERKSHIRE · ENGLAND

British Library Cataloguing in Publication Data

Mumford, Alan
  Making experience pay.
  1. Management
  I. Title
  658.4   HD31   79-42645

  ISBN 0-07-084536-0

12345 WM 83210

PRINTED AND BOUND IN GREAT BRITAIN

Contents

Preface

I have written this book from strong convictions about the reality of a manager's life, and about the nature of the learning opportunities available to him within it. I believe that too much of the guidance given to managers on how to learn has been based on an idealized model of managerial behaviour far removed from the responsive crisis style which many managers use. It seems to me more helpful to advise managers on how to learn in their actual environment than to tell them how they might learn in an ideal environment.

It is also my experience that managers have been given too narrow a view of the kind of opportunities available to them, with a succession of teaching techniques—case studies, T-groups, action learning—pressed as uniquely appropriate. There is, in fact, a range of situations from which managers may learn. Most opportunities occur on the job but few of them are used. I show how they can be used, while still giving priority to the results a manager is expected to achieve. I believe learning situations do not have to be manufactured; they already exist as part of the normal environment.

The thrust of the book is to give direct help to managers, and particularly to help them to manage their own learning. I have tried to do this not only by illustrating the opportunities available, but by helping the individual manager to understand his own learning style. Those of us in the business of helping managers to learn have given far too little attention to differences in the ways in which individuals respond to particular kinds of learning experience. I have tried to help managers relate their uniqueness as individuals to the diversity of learning opportunities and methods available to them.

I have given particular emphasis throughout to the ways in which a manager can identify and meet his own learning needs. I call the manager who is really capable of defining and working on his own learning needs a 'self-directed learner'. I do not intend to decry the help he can receive from others when I say that there is a need to shift the balance of discussion from the provider of learning to the manager. This is not to say that the manager does not need help on learning, but that he needs a different kind from that provided by many advisers and bosses. He also needs to understand more about what being helped means; it is one of the unusual features of this book that instead of suggesting ways in which advisers can help managers by designing learning experiences, I have described ways in which managers can better manage their own response to help.

The predominance of the masculine gender in the book might cause some people to assume that I am writing only for men, or do not recognize the existence of women managers. Neither is the case, but as it is probable that only between two per cent and five per cent of the managerial populations in the UK and USA are women, I have accepted that male descriptions will be most helpful to most of my readers.

This book would not have been written without the encouragement of my wife, the forbearance of my children and the help of Peter Honey.

1. The manager and his environment

Learning

Winston Churchill is supposed to have said that he was always willing to learn, although he did not always like being taught. I have known many managers with a similar attitude, and the most important point to make at this stage is that learning is not the same as being taught. Learning—the acquisition of knowledge and skills—is achieved in a variety of ways in managerial life. The details of my definition of learning will be found in chapter 4, but what I say in this and the next two chapters is based on the view that managerial life offers more opportunities for learning than it does for being taught.

The manager—a definition

I do not regard it as crucial for the purposes of this book to have a very tight definition of a manager. A manager is responsible for securing appropriate results with the help of people who work for him. This definition covers people who would be called supervisors, not managers, in industry—and also directors. It also covers people in professions who might not see themselves as managers—senior partners in professions such as accountancy or architecture, administrators in hospitals or social work, senior civil servants. The differences between these jobs are large, but they all have at least some managerial elements, which may in fact be the dominant features of the jobs. This is not to say that I regard the precise nature of the elements of management to be the same in all managerial jobs; as I will show in the next chapter, generalizations about what managers do are suspect. In fact, I take the view that what managers do is very much influenced by a number of factors in the environment in which he is managing; as will be seen later, I think that the demands on a manager are contingent upon the situation in which he is working, and that a manager's effectiveness cannot be defined in some ideal terms, but only in relation to his particular situation.

Why look at the manager's environment?

Most books or articles dealing with how or why managers learn seem to me to have missed some very important factors influencing or explaining the how and

1

the why. They have given insufficient attention to factors within the organization affecting the manager's interest in learning, such as cultural beliefs about learning, or change and conflict within the organization. Some reference may be made to the manager's boss, as an influence on his motivation to learn or as the carrier of a coaching responsibility. Few references are made to a man's colleagues as helping or hindering the creation and development of a learning environment. All these are failures to comprehend the true nature of the manager's environment as it influences his willingness to learn. But there are other aspects of his environment not referred to at all, presumably because the manager is seen solely as a relatively inefficient mechanism within a work context, rather than as a whole man who lives both inside and outside the work environment and is open to learning experiences at times other than working hours.

The case for looking at the manager's environment as part of the process of looking at learning needs and actions on learning is therefore that it is important to see the manager as part of a system, in which actions and interactions affect managerial learning needs, and in which learning needs take a wider and more realistic place than would be indicated by some of the narrow approaches to identifying needs.

Finally, it should be noted that a manager's environment is not fixed and immutable. It is constantly changing in response to a variety of pressures, just as the physical nature of the surface of the world changes. This is especially true of the social and technological environment in many industries; more immediately, it is true of the boss and colleague environment in which a manager works, as they change in person or in behaviour. We will be looking at the impact of a number of these changes.

The range of influences on the manager at work

The strongest influences on what a manager is required to do, on what he needs to do effectively, and therefore on what he has to learn are found at work. Charles Handy, in his admirable book on organizations,[1] identified over sixty different variables influencing the effectiveness of the organization; the effective manager has to be capable of handling these variables. From the point of view of the manager, it is likely that some things affect him more directly and potently than other things, which may be equally significant in determining what he does, but over which he has little influence. While few people would now accept the dominance of the type of technology on organization systems as advanced by Joan Woodward, there is no doubt that the manager's job differs in a highly automated, mass process plant from that in a craft-dominated, unit product factory. Yet technology expresses itself in a number of factors much closer to the manager, and it is these factors which determine in immediate terms what he does and how he does it—and therefore influence his motivation to learn. Since, in addition, it is an unusual manager who can cope with the visual picture of (let alone the concepts involved in) sixty or more variables, I use the following diagram (Fig. 1.1) when I am talking about influences on the manager's job. I will be taking up a number of these factors during this book; this chapter will look particularly at the influence of boss, collegues, the reward system, and the type of organization on the manager's need to learn and his motivation to do so.

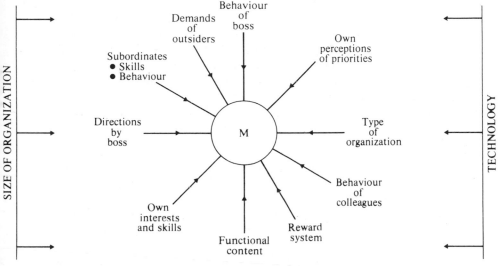

Fig. 1.1. Influences on the job of a manager

The boss as an influence on the learning manager

Some research in the American General Electric Company is often quoted to illustrate the importance of a man's boss in his experience of learning. When asked what was the most significant learning experience of their career, working for a good boss was the answer most frequently given. This response seems to me at least as likely to indicate the poverty of the other learning experiences through which these managers had passed as to really testify to the unique power of the boss. Some bosses do give a creative learning environment to their subordinates, in ways which I will describe later in the book (see especially chapters 6 and 7); many bosses do not. One particular weakness—the failure of bosses to act as effective coaches—has been noted and frequently written about in recent years. I have written elsewhere[2] about the problems of trying to force a coaching approach on managers whose basic managerial style is antithetical to the style required for effective development of their subordinates. It is my experience that only a minority of managers have the appropriate style, the collection of behavioural actions appropriate to this coaching. It is similarly a minority, and not necessarily the same people, who get substantial pleasure

3

from the wider, non-personal range of activities involved in successful development of others; they may get their pleasure from making organizational arrangements rather than from direct interaction in a learning sense with their subordinates. W. G. Bennis asked[3] whether for many managers it was enough 'to experience the epiphany of successive vicarious parental triumphs'. The learning manager will, indeed, find few bosses capable of or seriously interested in the development of their subordinates. I do mean seriously interested; there are quite a lot of bosses prepared to allow someone else to help their managers to learn, particularly where such efforts have the support of other powerful figures in the organizational hierarchy (a point explored later in the chapter). Apart from any direct contribution, the boss is, of course, likely to be the most important component both of the general climate about the desirability of learning, and of the specific environment, rewarding or punishing a manager for applying new skills or knowledge.

My analysis of bosses who are good conscious developers of their subordinates has shown that they have most of the following behavioural characteristics:

- They draw out the strengths and weaknesses of their subordinates rather than suppressing them
- They reward their people both materially and psychologically for the risks they take in attempting to develop themselves
- They positively seek to identify learning opportunities for their subordinates
- They give personal time to the development of subordinates—for example, in reviewing and analysing an activity for learning purposes
- They involve their subordinates in some of their own important tasks (not just 'delegate' Mickey Mouse tasks)
- They share some of their problems and anxieties with their subordinates, in the interests of their subordinates' development rather than simply as relief for themselves
- They listen rather than talk
- They do not say or imply 'be more like me'
- They take risks on the desired results of their unit in pursuit of relevant learning opportunities for their people.

In my experience, there are very few managers who are prepared to behave in this way (and who themselves work in an environment which would reward them if they did). Thus, there are very few bosses who are providing an appropriate learning environment. As I have just suggested, part of the explanation is in the organizational culture in which the bosses themselves work (and I will look at this point later in the chapter). Another part must be in the psychological make-up of the boss.

I believe that a boss who is a good developer of others must feel secure himself and be inclined to innovation and risk taking. However, not enough is known about the impact of these or other psychological characteristics on the way in which he might develop his subordinates. Clearly, if we had an analysis of a manager's behaviour on developer characteristics, and of his psychological profile, we would be able to develop more valid expectations of the learning environment he would be likely to provide. The assumptions that good managers will necessarily be good developers of others, and that we only have to explain to the good manager what he has to do, or coerce the bad manager into doing it—these assumptions form the basis (unstated) of many management development schemes. The assumptions are crass; they do not stand examination when tested against the reality of boss behaviour.

The reality for the learning manager will not surprise him, and can be dealt with once understood. He cannot depend on his boss to create or foster a learning environment for him; but the boss is only one part of the environment. If he has a boss who is a good developer, he should cherish and reward him.

My comments so far have been concerned with the conscious, positive role of the boss as a developer of others. Although, as I have shown, I am not as optimistic as some writers about the number of bosses who will be able to carry such a role, it is potentially part of the environment for many managers. All managers, however, have another kind of learning relationship with their boss, who is to a greater or lesser degree a model for them; his role as model may often be more influential than his role as developer.

Modelling is the process by which we observe the way others behave, and try to imitate them. I will be looking at the process of modelling in more detail later in the book. The important point to register here is that the boss provides a model in two different ways.

First, he inevitably and unconsciously gives his subordinates the opportunity to see how a managerial process is carried out—how he runs a meeting, how he deals with a difficult customer, how he plans and monitors the activities of his subordinates. He provides a model, and when he does something which his subordinate sees as successful, the latter may decide to incorporate that way of doing things into his own managerial behaviour. (He may also provide a negative model—an illustration of how not to do things.)

Second, the boss provides a model about the learning process itself. If the boss shows that he too is a learner, that he is looking for opportunities to add to his knowledge and skills, his subordinates may model their own beliefs and actions on his. (The same comment on his being a negative model applies.)

I will have more to say later in the book about the boss as model; this is a powerful and little understood learning process.

Colleagues as aids in learning

Since most forms of managerial work are conducted according to a competitive ideology covered by a veneer of cooperation, and since bosses, peers, and subordinates are constantly changing, real friendship at work is rare. Managers have colleagues at work, rarely friends. Colleagues, including subordinates, can provide a positive environment for learning:

- By providing models ('I wish I was as good at running meetings as David')
- By providing examples ('That experience in marketing seems to have helped Jack')
- By providing a demonstration of the effectiveness of a course in improving managerial skills ('Nobody can slip a phony definition of a problem past Tom since he went on that course')
- By (rarely) providing accurate and useful feedback to an individual about his performance ('I noticed you ended with the points against, and it seemed they stuck in the director's head instead of your positive points').

Unfortunately, the positive use of colleagues in this latter form is seen as difficult, for reasons of status, self-esteem, and competition. In chapter 8 I will be suggesting ways in which managers can use colleagues to enhance learning experiences, and limit the risks in doing so.

Colleagues can also provide a negative learning environment: the model of behaviour they give can be inappropriate or impossible for someone else to copy; they may not demonstrate the virtues of different kinds of career experience; they may be poor exemplars of what can be learned on courses. In this last case, their negative impact can be extremely powerful, in two ways. They may return from a course proclaiming loudly that it was a waste of time and that they learned nothing from it. Such statements make it difficult for others to show an interest in the same kind of learning experience, even when allowance is made for the manager making the comment. As Mandy Rice Davis said about a public figure who denied knowing her: 'Well, he would say that, wouldn't he'. Probably more hurtful is the manager who comes back from a course concerned with specific skills, and who demonstrates that he is no better than he was before.

Although this book is directed at the individual manager, learning is not necessarily a solitary process, clutched secretively to the bosom of the individual. Just as managers can learn from colleagues, they can learn with them, and indeed there is substantial evidence of the greater impact and implementation of learning when it has been undertaken in or by groups of colleagues. Part of the power of learning experiences like the managerial grid or Kepner-Tregoe decision making is that colleagues will often (not always) support each other in employing the new skills or techniques, thus helping to overcome one of the major problems of learning, the transfer from acquisition of a new knowledge or skill to implementation. In contrast, for a variety of reasons, an individual manager who brings a new technique into a group of colleagues who have not been trained in it faces at best a neutral and probably a hostile environment for the application of his new knowledge.

The influence of organization structure

The structure of systems and objectives of the organization in which the manager works influences his learning patterns because the nature of the

6

organization is one of the things which determines what a manager needs to be able to do effectively, and therefore what he needs to learn. An organization structure built to serve the purposes of a company with mature products serving stable markets, with predictable and not very intense competition, is likely to need quite different forms of managerial behaviour from that encouraged in an organization structure set to meet the needs of a burgeoning technology, constantly changing products, and fierce and often novel forms of competition—for example, in the pocket calculator market. In the steady-state organization hierarchy, regularity, agreed levels of authority, and formal methods of communication exist and set the demands on managerial skills. In the turbulent organization, the demands for speedy and effective action produce organizational arrangements which are less hierarchical in form, less neat and regular, less understood by those who work in them. Perhaps the most extreme form of this latter structure is the matrix organization, with dual reporting relationships, shared accountabilities, and constantly changing decisions about priorities and resources.

The subject of what causes, and what makes effective, different kinds of organization structure is outside the scope of this chapter. The important point for the learning manager is to recognize that what he has learned in one organization may not be appropriate in another, and that what he has learned in the existing organization may cease to be appropriate as the problems and opportunities faced by the organization change. (Charles Handy's two books[1,4] give fruitful analyses of some of the differences, although not all managers will appreciate the classical allusions with which he dresses up his analysis.) If he recognizes the changed situations he faces as he moves jobs or as he sees his existing organization change round him, the manager may see also both new learning needs and new learning opportunities. I can illustrate this from the following case.

A high technology company was faced with the problem of designing and launching a new range of products. The products, although basically similar to their existing range, offered new dimensions of speed and throughput. The products were interactive, so that the development of one depended on the effective development of another. As the new products were evolved, there grew increasing pressures on the existing organization structure with its straightforward separations between design, production, and marketing. Significant difficulties grew up in allocating resources between current and new products. The familiar bases for decision making—budgets, rules, separate accountabilities within a compartmentalized structure—could no longer cope with the new situation. New organizational patterns were created which redefined organizational relationships, broke up the hierarchical examination of problems, and set up power bases outside the control of the line executives. Among the results of these changes was the bewilderment of many managers who had operated successfully in the old environment but who found that the skills and approaches they had acquired to meet their old objectives within the then structure were no longer effective. They were used to working in a vertical organization, and thinking vertically. Now they had major lateral relationships in the organization, had to think laterally (and indeed were encouraged to read Edward de Bono). Managers used to managing cost centres now found themselves in charge of profit centres. Some, but not all, were able to cope with the demands of the new structure. They learned slowly and painfully, because the nature and results of the organizational change were not spelled out, and because there was insufficient recognition of the learning that was necessary.

The impact of organizational structure on learning needs is, of course, one step removed; it expresses itself through explicit or implicit demands on how a manager should behave; these demands are reviewed in the next two chapters.

The influence of organizational climate

I use the phrase 'organizational climate' to refer to what is sometimes less formally expressed as 'the way things are around here'. Climate is a condition, a set of usually unstated rules for behaviour. A sporting analogy is found in the game of cricket, in which a batsman is out if an umpire says he is. In some circumstances, he may have snicked a catch which the umpire cannot detect, and walk away, giving himself out—because that is the informal rule in the club for which he plays. The climate in other clubs might encourage quite different behaviour, such as rubbing your elbow or brushing your pads to indicate that no catch has been given. In the previous sections we have been looking at those objective factors in organizational structure and relationships which influence what, by logical analysis, a manager needed to learn. The organizational climate is what determines whether the logical analysis actually takes place and, if it does, whether any learning processes occur as a result. The climate encourages managers in learning when it is recognized that organizational objectives will be more effectively met if managers are helped to learn. Clearly, the climate discourages learning when that connection is either not present or has not been recognized.

The climate is expressed in both attitudes and actions. Here are four organizations with quite different climates for learning:

Organization A was a stable-state organization, with well established systems for management development. The top managers were recognized to have been through planned learning experiences on the way to the top, and were seen to contribute to the learning of others by the priorities they showed. One crucial event in establishing the climate was a decision that the manager in charge of the company's largest ever project should attend as planned a training course held in the first few weeks of his project. Questions about whether a manager could be released to attend a course were thereafter related to this decision.

8

Organization B had a stable, unchanged product, but decided to introduce a new organization structure with major new departments. The business had been based on creativity and selling rather than on effective management. The creation of new senior management jobs, occupied by insiders with little management experience, led to a partial recognition of the need to learn, but also to a great deal of insecurity about exposure of weaknesses. The learning climate was also uncertain because the top jobs were filled with people who themselves had no learning experience, and who were unsupportive of those under them.

Organization C was in a state of turmoil on technology, product, and organization. The objective need that the managers should be helped to learn how to cope with new requirements led to occasional consultancy initiatives and special learning events. The managerial climate was, however, sometimes punitive and often impatient—'If these guys don't know, we will bring in some who do.' The major changes in managerial requirements, though sought by top management and articulated by specialist management development advisers, were never translated into learning activities supported by top management. They were able to bring in the managers they needed for immediate business needs, and therefore felt no business pressure to develop the competence of existing managers to meet new needs.

Organization D had for some years been able to meet the needs arising from a modest growth in the business, largely by internal redeployment and promotion, with some external recruitment; it had not felt any need to help managers at middle and senior levels learn for their present or future jobs. The coincidence of three factors caused a change in the climate. It became increasingly clear that the same very small pool of managers was now the only resource for all senior appointments, some of which began to be made with a somewhat doubtful air; it became clear that there were few resources available for the planned future growth of the business, and it became clear that gaps in the experience and knowledge of some managers was inhibiting their performance. Because there was a degree of actual and potential hurt to the business reasonably attributable to past failures to plan and develop management resource, the managerial climate changed towards accepting the importance of examining managerial learning needs.

The organizational climate can be said to be favourable to learning when serious efforts are made by those in power to identify learning needs and do something about them. (Management development advisers are not normally powerful, although they may be influential. They do not create the climate, but merely adjust the temperature.) This means that they are then rewarding those who are trying to learn themselves, or are encouraging others to learn, which in turn creates a situation in which more people seek the rewards being offered; when the 'critical mass' of managers takes learning seriously, a climate has been created. Managers expend their energy on those activities which they expect to bring them organizational rewards, and avoid those which do not.

There are a number of aspects of organizational climate which determine *what* a manager should learn, rather than *whether* he will be encouraged to do so. Perhaps the most significant is the political aspect—the nuances of how decisions are made, and how people deal with each other in the process of making decisions. Whatever the formal structure, organizations work through a variety of informal networks, which may be particularly powerful. Knowing that a project will produce a given return on net assets employed may be less important than knowing to whom this figure is important and how important he is.

The managerial environment—complexity, conflict, and paradox

Managers frequently refer nostalgically to the days when organizational relationships were simpler, and when a manager was able to manage through the exercise of his own initiative and decision making. While it is surely the case that hindsight makes the position more simple than it was, managerial life probably has become more complicated and in the process has given added importance to certain dimensions of the manager's job, and therefore to some learning needs arising from managing in a more complex environment. To the extent that the manager ever did operate in a stable world, with organizational problems and styles of behaviour that were generally accepted, he does so no longer, because he works in conditions of turbulence and ambiguity.

In the UK, one of the significant changes has been in the balance of power between manager and managed, often requiring (but less frequently getting) a different approach to the process of decision making. These changed relationships have not yet led to drastic formal changes in organizational structure of the kind existing in Continental Europe and envisaged in the UK Bullock Report on worker representation on boards. If such changes are introduced, a major new learning need would be created, to manage effectively within the new structure. At the moment, managers are merely faced with recurrent problems of learning to manage in an environment where consent has to be sought and won. The problem is now so familiar that we seem almost to have forgotten that it represents a learning problem for managers, perhaps in the delusion that some change in legal arrangements will remove the need to handle the issue.

Rather than looking at this relatively familiar issue, it may be more interesting, and more useful, to look at other changing aspects of the managerial environment, and particularly at the ways in which working relationships between managers at similar levels in an organization are changing, and how this affects learning needs.

Complexity

Probably the most identifiable element here is the increasing influence of lateral, as compared with vertical, organizational relationships. The familiar, neat, hierarchical relationships down a management line, supplemented by dotted or different colour lines between staff or functional jobs still represent the norm, both in expectation and in actuality. Clashes of interest, priorities, and objectives across the organization and various forms of functional chauvinism have long existed but have been seen as peripheral, personal, or in some sense desirable. Yet divergencies of planning and purpose between design, sales, and production have been a recurrent organizational feature, and only relatively recently have they been seen as unnecessary and costly. Workshops or other learning events have been designed, to identify the nature of this problem and to secure commitment to working on it. The idea that these familiar dysfunctional aspects of organizational behaviour can be managed, and that managers can learn to manage them, is still, however, a relatively novel idea in some organizations.

A search for at least partial congruence of objectives and priorities between separate departments is unlikely in many cases to be resolved permanently simply by events in which managers learn how to manage existing departmental conflicts more effectively. There has therefore also been the development of structural changes in organizational relationships, in which lateral responsibilities are given as much significance as vertical accountabilities. Where the significance is given final organizational form by giving a manager two equal bosses, with a dual not a single chain of command (such as functional/product or geography/product), the result is a *matrix* organization. (Equality of power is what distinguishes this from the line staff relationship which may involve two bosses, one of whom, in practice, has primacy.) Managers who move, or are moved, into organizational structures of this latter kind may not recognize (among other problems) that they are faced with new definitions of what an effective manager does, and therefore with new learning problems.

Formal statements of changed organizational relationships are, of course, only the superficial aspects of the changed managerial environment. An article by S. M. Davis and P. R. Lawrence gives a view of one consequence which entirely coincides with my own experience of the reaction of managers to the introduction of a lateral addition to the organization structure:

> Some managers have the feeling they are not truly managing if they are not in a position to make crisp unilateral decisions. Identifying leadership with decisive action, they become very frustrated when they have to engage in carefully reasoned debates about the wisdom of what they want to do.[5]

A lot of managers identify with both the fact and the desirability of Harry Truman's notice on his desk: 'The buck stops here'. They find it difficult to cope when they are not sure where the buck stops.

Another consequence, identified by Jay Galbraith[6] for various forms of lateral relationship short of the pure matrix, is that influence is based on knowledge and information, rather than on status. This is a particularly devastating change for managers brought up to behave in the traditional way at meetings, where the information offered by subordinates is edited, bowdlerized, and otherwise transformed to suit what the boss wants to say. The learning problems faced by subordinate managers given the opportunity to influence events by revealing reality are considerable. The learning problem faced by their bosses in having to accept—and, indeed, to stimulate—an open exchange of information, losing the control previously afforded by their status, is in my experience even more pressing and more difficult.

Conflict

Galbraith says that the matrix 'institutionalizes the adversary system', and it is certainly the case that dual reporting relationships may have the consequence of introducing new forms of conflict. It was interesting to note, in a study which I carried out on the subject of conflict, that managers were more conscious of the conflict following a new organizational arrangement than they were of the conflict which preceded it. While this could be attributed in part to the impact of novelty, it was clear, in the discussions I held, that the issue was also one of learning to manage new kinds of conflict; managers recognized that they lacked the skills necessary to handle the conflict arising from the new organizational situation. They needed to have skills:

- To define and secure understanding of competing objectives and roles in a situation where line responsibilities were monitored by, and priorities influenced by, a powerful department reporting outside the divisional hierarchy
- To manage conflict as a positive organizational process
- To work on the interpersonal issues which accompanied the structural issues, in which conflict arising from what the 'interfering' department did was made 'worse' by the manner in which they did it.

Paradox

In this situation and others like it, managers are faced with a paradox which they find difficult to cope with. The paradox has two dimensions. The first is that only by clarifying and defining issues of priority and objectives can efficient trade-offs be made, choosing to carry out one activity first, allocating resources to this project rather than another. The additional dimension which creates the paradox is that, while conflict is sharpened through the clarifying process, the fact and necessity of interdependence is made more clear, requiring a sharing of information and commitment at some level to a consensus on what should be done. Ambiguity of objectives is replaced by ambiguity of authority. Understandably, managers find it difficult to behave in the way required by the paradox, which is alien both to the experience of most managers and to the natural tendency of many managers to simplify, especially on issues of 'who is to be master'. The learning needs which arise in this situation could only be

12

avoided if organization structures and the relationships between managers became less complex. The evidence is that this will not happen, that complexity, conflict, and paradox will be increasingly frequent factors in the manager's environment.

The familiar statement that a manager is someone who gets results through other people will more frequently have a qualification 'who are not under his organizational control'—with all the implications that has for the skills he has to learn. This means more subtle political behaviour rather than coercive-power-based hierarchical responses to the need to get things done.

The manager at home

Henry Longhurst, for many years golf correspondent for the *Sunday Times*, used to try and put the final crucial moments of open championships into perspective: 'A man may miss a three-foot putt on the last hole and still be an excellent husband and father'. While it is the objective of this book to help managers to sink the equivalent of the three-foot putt, the story does have another exceedingly pertinent message. Managers do not simply exist as individuals during working hours; their lives during time away from work are largely unstudied yet are very important for at least some of them in influencing at least the wish to be, if not the practice of being, a learning manager. Whatever the differences which may exist between the manger at work and the manager at home, any attempt to look at his interest in learning to be more effective must look at both lives.

I do not propose to look at the early lives of managers and to review the family processes which influence their psychological make-up and motivation to learn. While this early history is certainly important in helping to determine the way in which a manager will approach as an adult both the prospect and the actuality of learning experiences, it is history. Understanding his personal history might help the manager in a number of ways, but in terms of learning experiences as a manager there are a large number of more immediate influences which, if understood, are more likely to provide a concrete base for action. Some aspects of early family experience—competition in learning or achievement with parents, brothers, or sisters, the psychological and material rewards given by parents for risk taking, for academic achievement, for the pursuit of new experiences—are powerful agents on the young person and may be carried forward to the adult manager. His behaviour as a manager, and his attitude to learning are, however, likely to be determined by his immediate environment and his previous adult experiences in jobs relevant to his current job. Where managers refer to their early learning experiences and claim that these have been carried forward into adult life, it seems to me most likely that in adult life they have continued to be rewarded for learning practices similar to those they remember from their youth; without such adult rewards their early learning experiences would be simply memories rather than current practices.

For most managers, the primary non-work influence is the current home rather than the early home, and in the majority of cases the influence is that of a wife. (Regretfully I have excluded references in this chapter to husbands of managers.) This statement, of course, begs the question of what the nature of the influence is—how significant it is to what managers actually do. Unfortunately, there is remarkably little evidence on this; the absence of much serious study is probably another reflection of the unreal basis of so much that has been written about mangers. The absence of study is only explicable if the manager is seen as living two separate lives, interacting only in an economic or sexual sense. It could be true that a manager's behaviour at work is largely uninfluenced by his home life, but that is a proposition which at least ought to be tested. Although managers do not, in my experience, talk much at work about the influence of their wives on their careers or motivation to learn, the absence of comment is neither surprising nor illustrative of what the real position may be.

Certainly, the manager who is sufficiently awake to the possibilities of learning to be reading this book should be helped to see himself in the context of his domestic life, to understand both the difficulties and opportunities which exist there to influence his attitude to learning.

The absence of serious study might not be thought so surprising in the general context of the place of women in society, and of wives as submissive partners in marriage. Yet there is a volume of both literary and anecdotal evidence to suggest that at least some wives exercise a considerable influence on their husbands' attitudes to their careers and therefore on their motivation to learn. Both literary and anecdotal evidence may of course be emphasizing isolated and dramatic instances rather than the norm, which is why we need more research evidence.

Anecdotal evidence is by its nature highly individual, but is consistent in identifying some wives as major factors influencing the careers of their husbands, either positively or negatively. Thus it will be said of manager A that he was constantly pressed by his wife to look for advancement or new opportunities, and of manager B that he was held back by a wife who did not want to move home and who insisted on his regular presence in the family circle at the expense of the credit he might have received for working late. These examples of wifely influence are by no means uncommon, but they are basically examples of the influence of a wife outside the work environment. The more dramatic examples, usually offered in a form which would be called gossip if engaged in by females at home rather than males at work, are those where wives actually enter their husbands' territory. The territory is not the office but a dining room or dance floor, on these occasions transformed into a meeting-place between home and work. Here wives 'do their best' for their husbands. In the most acceptable form, this consists simply of looking attractive, sounding reasonably but not challengingly intelligent, and generally seeming an appropriate consort. In its more dramatic and less acceptable form, wifely behaviour can be seen as clearly attempting to influence her husband's career in a more positive way, not by demonstrating her own suitability as consort but by placing her husband's name more clearly before those in authority. These extreme (and, it must be said, unusual) forms of wifely behaviour clearly demonstrate a commitment to the furtherance of the husband's career, and suggest that such wives are potentially powerful agents in encouraging their husbands to take the necessary steps, including taking learning opportunities. (The question of how far some wives will go in helping their husbands' careers is one which has attracted more attention in novels than is justified in my experience by fact.)

On the whole, I see the main influence of wives on the manager's interest in learning as being on:

- His general level of motivation to succeed, to make progress, to acquire the visible indicators of success, to pursue a career
- His willingness to give greater weight to his participation in work issues than to participation in the life of the family, or in domestic or social duties or interests
- His willingness to undertake career moves which mean physical moves of home, perhaps to relatively less attractive locations.

Before looking at these, however, it is worth looking at the lesser but more direct influence of the wife on his ability to learn from on-going experiences at work. Unlike boss or colleagues at work, the wife offers a way of discussing issues without losing credibility with those who may affect his performance or his future at work. Although not all husbands want to reveal uncertainties and feelings of insufficiency to their wives, some will do so, and in the process of sharing may see issues in a more reassuring perspective. This may not, of course, be helpful to learning. In some cases, however, the process of exposing issues and talking about them helps a manager actually to define better what the problem is, and therefore helps him to identify some actions to deal with it. He may identify a learning need without his wife having made a conscious or direct input at all, other than seeming to listen and making sympathetic noises. In some cases wives do make a more direct contribution, perhaps at a stunning level of simplicity— 'If you think you aren't using the figures very well, couldn't you get someone else to go over them with you, and explain how you could use them better?' There are other occasions when a wife can help her husband understand the interactions in which he is involved by discussing them with him, or can help by discussing the advantages and disadvantages of a particular course of action, or by reviewing with him what has happened as a result of a particular action and discussing what he might do next time.

There are instances, too, of wives who are able to help their husbands by enabling them to rehearse particular arguments or a speech in advance of the work occasion. They may make pertinent comments about content or delivery, a direct learning experience for the manager. It is, I believe, much more rare for a wife to be asked to read a report prepared by her husband.

While the role of wives as listeners and sounding boards is fairly well recognized, on the whole I believe the direct role of wives in providing situations in which managers can learn to be more effective is under-recognized and under-utilized. Of course, the manager does have his male role and dignity, as he perceives them, to maintain; he may not relish the prospect of sharing a relative weakness with his wife. It is also true that not all wives are capable of assisting their husbands to learn, either through technical incapacity to offer help and advice in an acceptable form, or because wider problems within the marital relationship prevent a useful exchange.

Companies, which make both explicit and implicit demands on the wives of their managers, do nothing to equip them to help their husbands. In part this is because wives are expected to help only at the social level, and by being prepared to move house. In part it is because wives have never been thought of seriously as people capable of helping their husbands meet the real demands of their jobs, and therefore to help them learn. The only serious attempt to involve the wife in her husband's learning occurs on some senior executive courses, where wives are brought in, usually on the last few days of the programme, and are exposed to similar processes of learning so that they will know what their husbands have gone through.

Marriage and a manager's career

According to the Pahls, 'It seems sometimes as though the American company is in league with the wife in a joint endeavour to make a man work harder . . . By contrast, British managers prize and British firms respect the privacy of the home and the clear separation of home and work.'[7]

Where wives want their husbands to have a growing and increasingly successful career, they do so for reasons which are a mixture of the wife's own interests and of her involvement in the interests of her husband. A wife may be interested because she gains from the material rewards and status her husband's career brings, for the reflected glory which may be involved, for the additional justification created for her original decision to marry this particular man. She may also be interested because of her involvement in her husband's satisfactions, and her knowledge of the enjoyment which he will get from both career progress and the changing content of his job. Such wives will tend to encourage the husband in his motivation to succeed, and will accept and protect him from some of the consequences of career decisions which are inconvenient in family terms. These consequences may include changes in location, a decision to take up formal studies at home or at night school, or a routine of bringing work home from the office and disappearing into the study (or taking over the dining room). Not surprisingly, the Pahls in their research found that when a manager is faced with a job change involving a move of home, he thinks of the job content, whereas his wife thinks in terms of friendships, schools, and shops. Presumably the particular balance of who thinks most strongly about what is influenced by the particular stage of family growth—e.g., the difference

16

between newly-marrieds without children, and a couple with children at particularly vital ages for school purposes.

In these cases, the wife is helping to provide the environment in which the manager's motivation to learn in order to satisfy their joint ambitions is given significant encouragement.

It is also the case that wives can provide an environment which is at best neutral and at worst positively discouraging to career growth, and therefore to learning motivation. Not all wives are prepared to be placed themselves, or to have their family placed, as secondary issues in the marriage to the man's career ambitions. Indeed, it is my experience that there are an increasing number of marriages in which not only would the wife place inhibitions on career decisions affecting adversely her view of family needs and interests, but the husband would not, in fact, make the proposal in the first place because of the strength of his own feelings about the appropriate balance. In this situation, the influence we have so far been analysing as the wife's influence becomes swallowed in the larger issue of the marriage as a shared and sharing relationship.

The trend seems to me quite clear; wives as individuals will be less prepared to surrender their own interests to those of their husbands. For some wives, of course, the clash will be the more dramatic because it will be the wife's job and career interests which clash with those of her husband. The Pahls found that their job was relatively unimportant to wives, even though 50 per cent in their study had jobs. Cases of career clash will continue to be a minority, although I expect it to grow, simply because the pressures causing women to be wives and mothers first will remain heavy.

There can be no doubt, however, about the shift in cultural expectations (at least in the UK and the USA), legitimizing the wife's perception of her own interests, and changing the husband's view of her legitimate interests. Some marriages will have battles about whose interests will have primacy; other marriages will reach an accommodation of priorities. The accommodation will inevitably mean not only that the husband is less of a free agent on issues such as career moves, but also probably that he is less free on more mundane issues, such as the hours he keeps at home. A husband who has agreed to share babysitting with his wife is not able to give single-minded primacy to opportunities at work; his inability to be flexible about hours of work may influence his own and others' perceptions of his dedication to the business. There is, as far as I know, no evidence on whether a manager with balanced interests between work and home may actually be more able to give the necessary emotional energy to learning than someone totally wrapped up in his business life. They may approach business life with greater freshness, and greater willingness to take the risks involved in learning. If he is really less dedicated to a career and growth, however, he loses one of the strong motivations for learning. More managers will find themselves obliged to challenge the picture of themselves as a resource to be exploited, as serious competitors in a career race. (It ought, of course, to be the case that a manager's career should be determined by the results he achieves rather than by the hours he puts in; but—as I show in chapter 2—the question of whether the manager behaves in the way in which managers are expected to behave creates its own reality.)

For the present, however, the influence of most wives still probably conforms to the Pahls' finding, that the majority of wives . . .

> . . . saw their role in relation to their husband's work as being essentially a supportive and domestic one and only a minority took a more positive part in his work life. The typical wife saw herself as someone who cares for the house and children while her husband is at work and who helps him to sort out his worries and relax when he comes to the nest in the evenings.

Not all husbands want a more positive environment than this, and some who do may have faced a wife such as the Pahls quote: 'Once my husband caught me out as he spent one whole evening talking about a project and asked me about it next day and I couldn't remember anything that he had said.' No doubt the husband felt annoyed and frustrated; it is more likely that he saw the occasion as a criticism of his wife than as a comment on himself and his ability to check whether he was communicating successfully—an experience which he might have used as a warning about his work skills as well as about his personal skills in marriage.

The manager who wants to learn should therefore look hard at himself within his marriage, at the kind of career decisions he may be faced with and how far he will share them with his wife, at whether he wants to involve his wife in his work problems and ask her to help him analyse and resolve them. It would be tempting to take this further, and to talk about the ways in which the manager learns about himself as a person within the marriage. To do so would take us outside the reasonable limits of this book; perhaps the relevant point is that a manager who is conscious of learning within his marriage may be able both to transfer two things to his managerial environment—learning about self, and learning about learning.

Friends and acquaintances

The nuances and subtleties of the English language are the curse of foreigners who study it and the delight of native observers of social processes. I propose to presume understanding of the different meanings of friend, acquaintance, and colleague. Only one of the reasons why the manager rarely has friends at work has similar strength in his social life—geographical mobility makes it more difficult for him to develop strong continuing relationships. In addition, whereas he spends a lot of time with colleagues at work, who could in other circumstances become friends, he has much less time with people outside work, who therefore often become acquaintances rather than friends. Indeed, perhaps the emotional energy managers put into their work may leave them with less than they need for their marriage, and with none at all for friendship.

Friends are, in any event, usually seen as unlikely to provide the kind of positive learning environment given by colleagues; their jobs and experiences tend to be different, the opportunities for modelling are social rather than managerial in form. They may provide exemplars in a career sense, and thereby provide an encouragement to learning, but I would have thought that this is rare. It is more likely that the role of friends in the manager's learning environment is a quite different one, much less related to his immediate managerial career or skill. It is, in fact, part of the proposition with which we started, the manager as a whole person. Friends may help a manager to learn to be a more pleasant and acceptable person; in itself a desirable process, its value for the manager is doubled in so far as it may help him to recognize that he can develop and call on a wider repertoire of behaviour than the one he customarily employs at work. The Pahls describe one manager:

> Mr Eastwell, then, values his friends because they make him feel that he is not only the aggressive, ruthless man which his work has made him; they reassure him of the continued existence of his gentler side, confirm his view of himself as a man who enjoys playing with his children as well as being a member of the board of directors.

My own experience of observing managers in action at work (in itself unusual) has not extended to observing them in their social or home life, and I know of no research which would confirm or otherwise whether managers behave differently at home or in social life as compared with work. Probably the answer is that some behave in a very similar fashion and some do not. I think it unlikely that in most cases the choice of behaviour is conscious, and equally unlikely that managers recognize how far they have opportunities outside work to experiment with and learn from forms of behaviour which could then be applied at work. How many managers consciously study their friends to see which ones are effective listeners and why? Do they look at their friends to see why some of them seem to be particularly successful in getting the best out of the people round them? I believe that some managers are influenced by the behaviour of their friends, that probably they are few in number, and that their learning is almost certainly unplanned and unconscious, not deliberately applied in their work situation.

Other environmental influences on managerial learning

It would be possible to cover a much wider range of factors in the environment influencing both whether a manager learns and what he needs to learn. I have not dealt with some of the larger-scale issues of the social environment in which a manager works—for example, the need to be able to handle consumer groups or local amenity groups. Nor have I touched on the influence of the general economic environment, particularly whether a prolonged period of low economic growth affects the creation of career opportunities and thus the motivation to learn. I have not brought in the implications on motivation to learn of a low-differential, high-tax managerial group, as UK managers are encouraged to see themselves. Nor have I referred to the impact of technology—for example, in causing managers to learn about management information systems. I would have liked to write more about the impact of changes in the balance of power and of attitudes to authority within organizations, because these have a direct impact on the manager's ability to manage in the sense of making individual arbitrary (although perhaps effective) decisions.

I have preferred to deal instead with those influences which touch the manager most directly, and especially those to which he is more likely to be able to adapt in pursuing a learning objective.

Lost opportunities

This chapter has looked at the manager in the widest context, and has attempted to show the range of influences on his opportunities to learn. Many of these opportunities are not recognized and used; this is a theme which will be developed further when we turn in chapter 2 to the manager in the context of his job.

Questions

1. Which of the influences mentioned here do you think most powerful in your own case?
2. Are there some influences which you think you have not recognized fully in the past?
3. What actions might you take now?

References

1. Handy, Charles B., *Understanding Organizations*, Penguin, 1976.
2. Mumford, Alan, 'Management development—with or without the boss', *Personnel Management*, June 1975.
3. Bennis, W. G., 'Chairman Mac in perspective', *Harvard Business Review*, September 1972.
4. Handy, Charles B., *Gods of Management*, Souvenir Press, 1978.
5. Davis, Stanley M. and Paul R. Lawrence, 'Problems of matrix organizations', *Harvard Business Review*, May–June 1978. Reprinted by permission of the *Harvard Business Review*. Copyright © 1978 by the President and Fellows of Harvard College. All rights reserved.
6. Galbraith, Jay, *Designing Complex Organizations*, Addison Wesley, 1973.
7. Pahl, J. M. and R. E., *Managers and their Wives*, Penguin, 1972.

2. The manager and his job

In order to improve a manager's ability to perform effectively—whether through learning or some other process—it is necessary to define what he is doing, and what he ought to be doing. The previous chapter looked at the wide range of influences on the manager and his job. This chapter will review what managers actually *do* as a result of those influences. This analysis will show that traditional theories have led to unhelpful definitions of learning needs, and that managers should not be asked to learn solely managerial skills appropriate to the rational, orderly world of textbooks, with neat boxes and divisions of skills; they should be helped also at the level of the disorderly world which is the reality of many managerial jobs.

The problem of generalization

Winston Churchill described Russia as a mystery wrapped in enigma inside a puzzle. Managerial jobs seem to me to have the same characteristics. For understandable reasons, many of the attempts to specify what managers need to learn in order to be effective have had highly standardized results. Differences of emphasis have been caused more by the personal skills and prejudices of management teachers, and by the norms of a teaching environment in favour of intellectually respectable analyses, than by differences of view about the nature of the jobs of managers. An emphasis on quantitative analysis or interpersonal skills, on managerial teams or corporate strategy, is selected from general statements about what managers do, rather than from rigorous analyses of what particular managers do in particular environments. Whatever its merits as an economic approach to the problem of dealing with numbers of managers in a teaching environment, there is no doubt that it leads to a poor match between the learning experiences provided and the learning opportunities actually needed by individual managers.

Given the variety of influences on the manager as a person, and on the results expected of him, as illustrated in the previous chapter, it is not surprising that what managers actually do varies considerably, and that their learning needs also vary. It is important, therefore, that the individual manager should be helped to understand the real nature of his own job, instead of being offered general statements, often couched in terms which have no contact with recognizable managerial behaviour. Oscar Wilde's aphorism 'Truth is never pure and rarely simple' applies both to the problems managers are required to answer and to the total problem of defining what managers do.

Classical management theorists

One of the major problems in identifying the reality of managers' jobs has been the popularity—certainly in management education and consultancy—of early statements about the elements of management. The first attempt to generalize, that of Fayol, encouraged an approach which, though it attracted the label scientific, was scientific in its superficial appearance of rules, regularity, and order, rather than from any association with scientific processes of arriving at those statements. He saw the following as the elements of management:

- Forecast and plan
- Organize
- Command
- Coordinate
- Control.

Later authors, such as L. F. Urwick and E. F. L. Brech, continued the theme of all-embracing statements, of authoritative rules, emphasizing aspects such as the span of control, the manager as motivator, and the manager as integrator. Brech's switch of verb from *command* to *motivate* was an indication of the impact of the human relations school mentioned below. The problem represented by these writers, and by many others who have followed them in print or lecture, is that interesting conceptual models, undoubtedly based on personal experience, became accepted as statements of generally applied reality rather than being seen as statements of prescription. As statements of prescription, they suffer from the grave defect that they do not touch closely enough the reality of the manager's job, either as he actually performs it or—more importantly—as he perceives it. For the reality is that managers do not perform their jobs according to large-scale verbs such as organizing, nor do they conceptualize their activities so that they recognize themselves as at separate times directing, motivating, or integrating.

The attractiveness of these statements to generations of management students can be explained partly by the absence of any other analyses of their work, and partly by the apparent simplicity of understanding involved in being given five, eight, or ten verbs describing the manager's job. Since simplicity was accompanied by a degree of intellectual respectability, the attractiveness of these statements to those in the businesses of management education and consultancy is readily understood, since both are able to maintain their business only by having recognizable packages of convenient size and bearable weight.

The manager as aura

The popularity of the next conception of the manager's job can presumably be attributed in large part to the models apparently provided by the Second World

War. As a result of this experience it was natural that managers should be seen primarily as administrators and leaders. The two strands were never entirely happily woven together, since the manager as administrator could accommodate the rules and boxes of Fayol and Urwick, while the concept of the manager as leader focused on personal qualities and the ability to get things done. The job of the manager was seen as 'to get results through other people', and attempts to explain how this was achieved concentrated heavily on lists of personal qualities and later more 'scientific' psychological characteristics. In the process, the focus shifted from what the manager did to what the manager seemed to be as a person.

From the perspective of this book, the particular significance of this post-war development was expressed in the evolution of the Administrative Staff College at Henley as a major management education institution of significant reputation in the UK, which attempted until the middle 'sixties to combine both administrative and personal quality themes. Henley's use of biography as a significant feature on their main course was a revealing expression of the dominance of the view of the manager as a special quality of person, getting his results by the expression of what he was as a person, in what he did as a leader. The attempt actually to define the required qualities became so difficult that once the list passed one hundred, apparent simplicity came to the rescue again, and the word *charisma* was increasingly used to escape from the indefinable. From a learning point of view, tracking down and pinpointing generally applicable personal qualities such as leadership, decisiveness, judgement, initiative, proved as elusive as capturing mercury from a broken thermometer, because neither the list of qualities nor the definition of what was meant by them could be agreed. 'Qualities' such as 'leadership' are defined quite differently by different people, and although attempts are made to train managers in leadership, the concept and approach is, in my view, a blind alley.

The manager as manipulator

At the same time as the 'personal qualities' school grew up, a combination of research in the American Hawthorne works and war-time experiences in which managers as officers were taught to show concern for their troops led to the view of managers as organizers of effective human relations. The job of the manager was to get the best out of the people working for him; the training method was to expose managers to a series of cases showing how a concern for the individuals working for you could be repaid in more effective production. Managers had adopted from family business owners a concern for the intimacies of the family lives of those who worked for them; inquiries on the state of the wife's back or Johnnie's scholastic progress were felt to give appropriate recognition to individuals, and to ameliorate the sordid requirement to get people to work harder.

The human relations wave is now regarded with some contempt, and undoubtedly was mechanistic, manipulative, and finally ineffective. Its significance for us now is that, whereas the classical and personality theories of management almost certainly did no damage, because they did not provide managers with tools they could use, the human relations approach has been unhelpful in two ways. While giving a useful initial boost to understanding of the significance of other people in the job of the manger, the human relations approach tended to deal in relatively superficial aspects of relationships with others, and to be condescending in its view of the kind of issues which a manager should discuss with his subordinates and how he should discuss them.

The manager as sensitive plant

The crudities of the human relations concept of the manager's job were replaced in the 'sixties by the much more subtle dimensions offered by the revelations offered through the analysis of interpersonal relationships. Instead of it being seen as the job of the manager to motivate others, in some sense to push motivation into them, it was now believed that it was his job to release motivations they already possessed, and to provide conditions in which their inherent abilities could be released. Douglas McGregor's *Human Side of Enterprise* was the original and most influential expression of this view. Like many other writers, he found it convenient to produce labels—Theory X Theory Y—for the general statements he made to explain what managers did. His immensely popular book has been widely used in management education and training; it may well have become a real influence on what managers do, but it is a prescription and not a description, a fact which McGregor himself noted wryly when he took on management responsibilities at Antioch University.

In terms of understanding the manager's job, the main contributions of the interpersonal relations school has, however, not been in the generalizations of McGregor but in the specific examinations of the group processes in which the manager is involved, sponsored initially through the confusingly labelled 'T-groups' and 'laboratory training', and later through more structured training experiences and through consultancy work with particular managerial groups. Although retaining an element of generalization—that interpersonal relationships are of major significance in any manager's job—the interpersonal school is also important because its method of working ensured that relationships were also seen in highly specific contexts—of particular person A with particular person B. The manager's job was now seen to contain a variety of forms of behaviour in relation to other people, behaviour which was specific, identifiable, and usable for a number of different purposes. Instead of dealing in conceptual categories, with all the problems of identification and translation—exactly what does a manager do when he is commanding or motivating—managers were helped to analyse individual behavioural acts, and to see the results of those acts. Thus managers began to understand, for example, that to behave according to an earlier stereotype of manager as leader, so that all the proposals in a meeting, all the direction, came from the single leader source, was not a sufficient or effective way of carrying out a manager's responsibilities.

The other major benefit from the attention given to the manager's interpersonal responsibilities was that it brought out what many would consider to be the dark side of the moon. Classical theory had certainly proposed a calculating rational man, pursuing his ends by the well controlled exercise of his intelligence. Now the other side was revealed—the extent to which emotions were involved, and that the manager needed to recognize and manage those elements, just as he did the more objective elements.

Reality arrives

It is an extraordinary fact that statements about the manager's job were for so long prescriptive in form and unscientific in origin. It seems now ridiculous that so many theories were erected telling the manager what he should do on the basis of so little information about what managers actually do. In terms of helping managers to learn, too much of the early work did not start from close enough to what the manger did. For the manager who wishes to understand his job in order to learn, the work of an Englishwoman, Rosemary Stewart,[1] and an American, Henry Mintzberg,[2] is crucial, even if he chooses not to read it. The uniqueness of their work was that they obtained detailed analyses of what managers actually do. The information they acquired was explosive because it showed that managers not only did not operate according to the concepts of the classical theorists, but were in fact not operating most of the time in any way consistent with a picture of them as rational organizers of events, processes, and time to meet organizational or personal objectives.

The special feature of Rosemary Stewart was that she reported findings about managers based on their having kept diaries about their work. (A Swede, Sune Carlson had used this method in 1951, but it had no major impact on the UK or USA—a familiar problem in scientific invention.) It has to be admitted that self-kept diaries clearly can be fallible, because of the difficulty of actually keeping accurate time records when you are a busy executive and of deciding under which heading to report an activity, and because of the possibility that the manager's decision on what to record could be affected consciously or unconsciously by a view of what he ought to be doing. Stewart, however, put her feet on a path which is of major importance, and started the process of concentrating on the reality of management work.

Stewart's first book was published in 1967; the title—*Managers and Their Jobs*—is itself a significant comment on what had gone before (and would have been the most appropriate title for this chapter if I had not wished to avoid plagiarism even in the title). As the title suggests, the book deals with the variety of managerial work, although she produced some typologies representing groups of managers. The data used was obtained by getting managers to

25

complete daily diaries on forms designed by the author. The diaries were analytical rather than anecdotal in form, using a series of headings. The main findings relevent to this chapter were :

- There were major differences in what managers did and how they did it
- An average working week of 42 hours concealed significant differences in the number of hours worked
- Informal discussions with other people took up half the time of many managers
- Time spent in formal committees was less than predicted for most managers
- There were substantial differences in how much time managers spent largely alone—the average was only one third of their time. Differences occurred not only between managers with different functional roles but between managers in the same function
- The 'normal' picture was of managers having only one half hour every other day when they would be totally undisturbed.

Stewart's work exposed some of the weaknesses in attempts to generalize about what managers do. Perhaps most crucially, her work joined that of Carlson in showing that the prescriptions of classical theory about what a manager should do were simply untenable in terms of how managers actually spent their time. The classical emphasis on activities requiring thought was out of key with the actuality of how little time managers spent alone, with the opportunity to think. (It is of course possible to hypothesize that managers are actually able to think at different levels simultaneously, and particularly that they can think seriously about one subject while others are talking. I know of no research which would support such a hypothesis, and the few managers I have met who would claim such an ability to be, in computer language, multi-programmed never demonstrated it to my satisfaction.) The absence of significant chunks of time capable of being devoted to thinking about major problems, rather than as discussion time or information-getting time, is indeed a research finding which is supported not only by my own experience as a manager and as an observer of managers, but by all the forms of anecdotal evidence which have come my way from discussion with other managers.

Since there is a risk of being misunderstood on this point, I should make it clear that I regard the way in which managers use their time as being quite frequently inefficient and inappropriate, both for their personal and for their unit objectives. In that sense, the classical prescriptions represent desirable goals. But it is only when managers have looked at the way in which they actually do their jobs, and have tested the congruence or otherwise of this with their objectives that meaningful improvement, development, or learning plans can be drawn up. Rosemary Stewart's findings do not represent the ideal, and they should not be used for exculpation; they represent an actuality, giving an opportunity for change. They also represent a kind of analysis which gives, as we shall see later in the book, the opportunity to identify concrete activities which can be changed.

Rosemary Stewart's second book[3] too had a title—*Constrasts in Management*—which underlined the theme of differences in the way managers perform their jobs. In the research she undertook before writing the book, her original diary-keeping approach was supplemented by questionnaires, interviews, mail records, and observation. In this book she developed a different series of typologies, based on the types of contacts maintained by the manager, his basic work pattern, and the relative difficulty of the relationships to which he is exposed. The essential finding is by now no surprise; there are substantial differences in what managers do, because the nature of their jobs differs markedly. The work pattern of a manager of the type she calls *systems maintenance* is represented by recurrent activities, a very fragmented day, and frequent trouble shooting. On the relationship dimension, she finds significant differences in what managers do, with variations on the kind and frequency of contact with boss, colleagues, subordinates, or customers.

I find that descriptive labels for types of manager are popular among managers, who like the simplicity of knowing that they are 9.1, or gamesmen, or Theory X. I am rather sorry that Stewart has introduced typologies—hub, peer dependent, and solo—because I feel that broadening the base for generalizing about managerial jobs does not really overcome the problems of generalizing in a useful way. Stewart has, however, made two other contributions which I consider very important, and especially significant for this book. The first point is her explicit recognition of the implications of her work for management training. Readers will now begin to recognize the theme in her words: 'Management training . . . tends to make implicit assumptions about work patterns that are inappropriate for helping managers who work in jobs with different types of work pattern'. Different job content means different learning needs.

Stewart's other contribution is one to which I will be turning in more detail in the next chapter. It is sufficient here to say that her analysis of jobs according to the *choices* available in them, the *constraints* affecting them, and the *demands* made on them is again an indicator of significant differences between jobs which will influence substantially the content of learning appropriate to those jobs.

Henry Mintzberg is another major original in the field of understanding managerial work. Whereas Stewart's original work was based on self-kept diaries, and her later work mainly on interviews, questionnaires, and diaries, with some observation, Mintzberg's own studies were based on his observation of chief executives at work. His findings are revealed in an article devoted to his own research,[5] and are expanded in his book.[2] Managers would probably find his *Harvard Business Review* article[5] the most persuasive and most useful, particularly because he incorporates in it parallel findings by other writers.

His first article ties in closely with Stewart's first book; most particularly in the range of differences he observed in how his chief executives used their time. The ranges he found over a week included:

27

—Amount of evening work   0–11 hours
—Amount of mail   112–230 items
—Number of activities   86–160
—Time on desk work   6.4–10.7 hours
—Time in scheduled meetings   10.6–29.8 hours
—Time in unscheduled meetings 1.2–9.6 hours

In his book, he uses his own research and that of others to establish this picture of managerial life:

- Most managers work at an unrelenting pace—the mail pours in, the telephone rings, and meetings are held. 'When free time appeared, ever-present subordinates usurped it.' He comments that pace and workload are due to the inherently open-ended nature of the job; the manager 'never has the pleasure of knowing, even temporarily, that there is nothing else he can do'
- Managers characteristically have brief, varied, fragmented contacts with people and issues; his own study showed his chief executives had 36 written and 16 oral contacts each day, nearly all dealing with distinct issues
- Half the observed activities were completed in less than nine minutes—only ten per cent took more than an hour
- Managers dealt with a diverse range of issues, with significant and insignificant issues interspersed in no pattern (an external public relations crisis, presentation to a retiring employee, bid for a new contract, office space).
- Managers pick up those elements of the job which are current, specific, and well defined, and those that are non-routine
- Managers prefer the oral to the written word—and spent (from various studies) 57 to 89 per cent of their time on oral communication.

It is worth underling the point that Mintzberg's own work was done with chief executives. Although he does not say so, it would be a natural assumption that chief executives in comparison with other managers, would be

- More in control of their time, since they had no boss to make demands on them
- More likely to be using large slabs of time for thoughtful analysis, because they would be less subject to the demands of operational fire-fighting
- More likely to be planning and looking ahead
- More likely to be dealing with strategic or priority issues.

Although more detailed studies would be necessary to prove the point, the picture produced by his observations can therefore be accepted as true for managers below chief executive with some confidence, even where it is not confirmed by other studies. The pressures at lower levels would be most likely to produce results even more strongly in the direction indicated by his observations.

Mintzberg concludes that similarities in managerial jobs outweigh the differences. This is not, I think, a particularly helpful conclusion, since it really only confirms that there is some sense in using one word, manager, to describe a collection of jobs. Although he argues that managerial jobs are remarkably alike, he agrees that there are differences related to personal characteristics or roles. The concept of roles is one I shall turn to later in this chapter. For the moment it is enough to say that Mintzberg too has shown that the job of managing, as it is practised rather than as it is preached, does not produce and perhaps does not require the kind of managers described by the classical theorists and apparently sought by many designers of management education or training. He confirms that the job of managing does not accommodate or develop people who sit back and plan reflectively; the job as normally practised demands and attracts people who are able to secure enough information for the purposes of immediate action, who adapt to quickly changing types of demands on a variety of personal skills, and who are able to respond quickly to the pressures and conflicts of events, events which the manager has often neither planned nor forecast.

Experiences of the manager's job

It may be necessary to add at this point that the concern I have is not to establish that the classical theorists were wrong in their analysis of what managers should do, nor that what Stewart and Mintzberg give us is a better analysis. Rather I am saying that as a basis for learning it is more useful and practical to start from where managers are, and to build the 'ought to' activities on as appropriate, rather than to ignore the realities and launch into learning how to do an idealized job, because the learning will quickly drain away under the impact of reality. My concern is to establish that until the existing real problems of managers, often at a relatively mundane level, are identified and dealt with, the higher-level analytical and thinking work—even if 'learned' on a course or through some other experience—will not be applied. Lengthy meetings without useful results are a frequent occurrence; until managers have been helped to identify the causes and deal with that problem, they are actually unable to do other kinds of work (even if they want to). Similarly, it is more relevant to identify the demands made on managers by telephone calls than to expose them to learning about computerized management information systems. If it is taken as axiomatic that it is the job of the manager to manage events, it ought to be a major preoccupation of the learning manager to manage himself and his time, rather than to allow others to do so. Yet, in my experience, managers find it very difficult to 'manage' telephone calls; one of the few occasions when I saw the telephone being managed was when locks were put on the telephones to prevent outgoing calls in the morning (the reason was, of course, one of economy, not efficient use of the manager's time).

The kind of information produced by Stewart and Mintzberg, although supported by other studies, can be criticized and dismissed on methodological grounds. The number of managers on whom the data is based is small, the validity of information collected by interview, diary, questionnaire, or observation can be criticized, and each of these methods has its own advantages and disadvantages.[6] The Stewart and Mintzberg findings are convincing to me because my own experience as a manager, as a subordinate, and as an observer of managers in action supports the essence of what they say, and often agrees in detail.

However, even the generalizations offered by Mintzberg, disposing of old myths, need to be taken cautiously. The pressures on the manager, the specific requirements he had to meet, have varied considerably in the organizations in which I have worked, and I have drawn upon some of this experience in chapter 1. In each organization, the unique features of what the manager had to learn in order to perform effectively in his particular job in that particular environment were at least as important as the generalizable features. To give an illustration, I will refer to one of the generalizations made by Mintzberg. He says that the achievement of effective working relationships with colleagues is a major part of the manager's job, and that for most managers this is a far more crucial activity than many of the standard descriptions of planning, decision taking, and delegating to subordinates.

When working with a group of senior managers in one of my organizations I observed the following feature of their jobs:

- Effective working relationships with colleagues were important, as the flood of organizational development material has insisted
- Different groups within the organization had different understandings of what was meant by 'effective'
- Different members of the same group had different views on what was effective.

The problem, therefore, of giving real meaning to the general job requirement of having an effective working relationship with colleagues was already considerable. It is worth special attention because, in this particular case, they were managing a process of considerable technological innovation, constantly encountering problems which they had not experienced before, and were responsible for drawing together discrete but highly interactive parts of one main product. Each manager was required to produce results in his area, but could only do so by ensuring that he stayed broadly in step with his colleagues.

The definition in concrete terms of this general job requirement was therefore a difficult task, which involved helping the group to recognize the need to move from positions of personal competition and retention of resources to a position of identifying shared goals and negotiation of resources. As with many managers, philosophies of competition, of the Win–Lose dynamic, had been learned and deployed. Scarcely had the group painfully identified for itself, and learned how to deploy, a more collaborative Win–Win approach than they were subjected to organizational pressures which required a new definition of effective working relationships. A new director imposed a different definition, thoroughly at odds with the remnants of English public school traditions which still influence English managerial behaviour. Those traditions are supportive of the view that you do not give openly adverse comments on the behaviour and performance of schoolmates or, in adult life, colleagues. Criticism may be implied, may even be offered with a show of reluctance in private, but it is not given in public except in the most desperate circumstances. In school life, the norm is that you accept unfair punishment rather than reveal the actual transgressor. Business life in the UK does not encourage managers to go quite so far, but in the particular environment I am describing, open criticism of the failures of colleagues even where these failures adversely affected your own performance was not part of normal behaviour.

The new director changed the definition of a significant part of his subordinates' jobs by requiring them to be open in public not only about their own problems and failures, but also about the problems caused by the failure of others. Only in this way, he felt, could he get at the problems in this highly interactive technology early enough to resolve them. This requirement, however, changed the job requirement of effective working relationships, so that managers were required to work effectively together not in a spirit of relatively unchallenging collaboration, but in a framework of collaboration achieved in a context of confrontation and challenge.

I have given this example at some length because it illustrates a number of points which are particularly important to the manager who is trying to analyse his job in order to learn how to be more effective.

- Specificity: the aspects of their jobs in which managers are required to be effective are specific rather than general. There is no Platonic ideal of what managers do
- Situational: the total situation produces a variety of pressures which give emphasis to particular features of the job
- Dynamic not static: the requirements in the job change with changing circumstances. Analysis of priorities, and of the crucial factors within a job, may be made invalid as circumstances change.

Even the improved understanding of what managers do offered by Stewart and Mintzberg needs to be taken further. They have produced their own generalizations which, although interesting and useful, can still be dangerous guides for the learning manager. As this illustration has shown, even if the general proposition that managers need effective working relationships with colleagues has been found valid for a particular manager or group of managers, the definition of what is effective will vary substantially. Unless the manager is helped to understand the particular definition which applies in his particular situation, any attempt, to help him to learn about effective relationships is at risk of failing either because it is couched in general terms, with the problems of transfer we will discuss later in the book, or because the specific learning is actually inappropriate to the real situation.

Representation and role

I turn now to an area of the manager's job which has been too little studied. Although writers like Stewart and Mintzberg have talked about different managerial roles, they have really been concerned with the different weighting of activities within managerial jobs—roles as leader, as representative. It is important here to talk about a different aspect of role, defined as the aggregation of generally expected forms of behaviour in a job.

I was participating once in a discussion about some of the problems faced by the firm in which I was then working. The discussion ranged over a number of issues, but gradually rose to heights of cerebral activity in which we castigated the board for lack of strategic thinking, failure to think in global product terms, and inability to define meaningful performance standards other than return on net assets. During a pause in which we contemplated the enormity of the attack we had launched (none of the directors, of course, was present), one of the participants coughed and said with a deadpan face and unemphatic voice, 'The real question is whether they could manage a piss-up in a brewery'.

The comment illustrated to me one of the issues about the manager's job. Managers are judged in significant part according to expectations by others of what the manager is supposed to do, and some of those expectations are geared to actions which are not in themselves managerial, but which are believed to represent effective managerial behaviour. It is the job of the manager not merely to do the right things, but to look as if he is doing the right things. He will look as if he is doing the right things if he matches the expectations people have of people in his position. Thus, one stereotype of managers is that they are people who take decisions, and that the decisions are made more effective because 'good' managers take the decision authoritatively rather than hesitantly. It is not enough that the manager actually takes a decision (although that is part of his role as manager); he must also look good while he does it (because that is another part of his role). Further, a manager will often take a decision quickly in order to demonstrate authoritativeness, although the objective job requirement will almost certainly be that he should make that decision which produces the best results—which probably means that he should think about the problem, ask for more facts, weigh and evaluate before announcing his decision.

After a selection interview on one occasion, the senior manager for whom I was assisting to select a subordinate, having reviewed the candidate's experience—all highly relevant—finally turned him down, saying 'I can't imagine him ever banging the table and telling someone they just had to produce the goods'. As this example shows, some actions by managers are not in themselves basically managerial, but represent something about being a manager. Anyone can bang a table—that is not explicitly a managerial skill; it can, however, be an expression of a managerial role requirement.

Sometimes, too, the expectations of the manager mean that he should behave in ways contrary to those which the objective requirements of the job indicate. It may be more important for him to seem to be doing the right thing than to be actually doing it, which is why managers will participate in schemes and approve policies so long as they do not have actually to undertake serious activities in connection with them. Thus managers will approve management development schemes, but will take no personal role in the development of their subordinates, or will accept the concept of corporate planning, but never use the results to manage activities. Another aspect of the clash between public expectations and objective job requirements is that it is more important to be seen to be doing something than to be doing something which is not seen. Thus it is more significant for most managers to visit the shop floor (the public, ambassador role) or to have a desk piled with paper (managers ought to look busy) than to have a clear desk, no visitors, and to be indulging in that most rare and most suspicious managerial activity—thinking.

What a manager does must therefore be seen not just in terms of its contribution to those results which would be defined as the desired consequences of his job, but in terms of apparently subsidiary activities which in fact also help to define the effective performance of role—activities which may have only a tenuous or low-priority association with the apparent major results desired in the job. Much managerial behaviour, in my experience, can only be explained in terms of its relationship to role expectations rather than in terms of its relationship to direct job requirements. Managers do things which they consider to be appropriate demonstrations of themselves as managers, so that they will look like managers.[7] Full diaries, long hours, desks crowded with paper, an office constantly occupied with meetings—these are all seen as necessary demonstrations of the manager's job. There is nothing indecent or inappropriate in this, until the stage is reached where form actually becomes more important than substance. Any analysis of the manager's job which leaves out those things which demonstrate the ways in which he performs the role of manager is incomplete, and will not lead to a fully rounded analysis of those things which a manager needs to do well in his job. The lack of attention to these aspects is another manifestation of over-concentration on the objective, rational features of managerial jobs. A manager needs to learn how to handle the public performance elements of his role as well, to manage consciously the interplay between appearance and reality, to see that the impressions he conveys about himself are compatible with the qualities he and others presume to be appropriate to an effective holder of his job. As Goffman puts it, a judge is supposed to be deliberate and sober, a pilot in a cockpit is supposed to be cool.[8] Doing is being. The presentational aspects can also be seen clearly in political life. It was said of Adlai Stevenson that he was too witty to be taken seriously as a Presidential candidate, and in the UK the apparent langour of Reginald Maulding not only became a caricaturist's joke but was felt to be quite out of key with the 'busyness' expected of a politician. In fact, he was just able to work more quickly than most of his peers and thus had time to look lazy. I have observed both these phenomena in business, with managers who did not regard it as worthwhile to conceal their true selves in the interests of a better managerial image of gravitas and dedication. They were suffering to some degree from role incompatibility.

There is, of course, no single role to be understood, perceived, or performed. There are many managerial roles, which are appropriate both to different jobs and to different facets within one job. In one company in which I worked, the role requirements appropriate to a particular group of managerial jobs changed, as priorities within the jobs changed. In order to be seen as effective managers, the job holders were required by the pressures applied by more senior managers to give more time to preparing plans, to reviewing achievements, and to deciding on the actions to be taken to improve achievements. The pressures applied, however, did not merely emphasize the objective requirements placed on managers but implied that managers would only be seen as meeting these objective requirements if they demonstrated the priority attention being given to them by holding meetings at unusual times. Thus there was a rash of planning and review meetings starting at 8 a.m., or 6.30 p.m., or on Saturday morning.

Appearance and reality

The manager's job must therefore be seen as containing not only activities which are clearly and directly associated with the task requirements in his job, but also activities more related to how he will be perceived. Too little attention has been paid—both in the general literature about managerial jobs and in the provision of learning experiences for managers—to the connection between objective job requirements and those role requirements which involve demonstration. Those role requirements which are about perception and appearance are also a form of reality.

As we will see in the next chapter, effective managerial behaviour embraces both the objective requirements of the job and the dramatic, demonstrative aspects. Managers continue to act in role, by demonstration, not only because that is in accordance with expectation, but because this behaviour is rewarded in a variety of ways by those at whom the behaviour is directed.

Summary

We know that what managers do in their jobs is the result of an extraordinary pot-pourri of influences, and that in even apparently similar jobs some managers will give more emphasis to some aspects than other managers do. Research and our own experience tells us that managers are far less dominated by the objective, rational, thoughtful processes of management than most books of management theory propose. We can also recognize that the way in which a manager presents himself, and meets views about his role, is an important aspect of his ability to do the job.

The manager who wishes to learn how to be more effective is more likely to do so if he starts from a basis of reality, and of specific requirements, than if he starts from generality. The learning manager ought therefore to analyse his job content, the ways in which he actually spends his time, and the ways in which he demonstrates himself as a manager. The ways in which he could do this are set out in the next chapter.

Questions

1. Which theories, books, or experiences have influenced your beliefs about the content of managerial jobs?
2. What do you see as the most important parts of your job?
3. Does the time you spend relate directly or inversely to those parts?
4. How could you collect more information about what you do and how you do it?

References

1. Stewart, R., *Managers and Their Jobs*, Macmillan, 1967.
2. Mintzberg, H., *The Nature of Managerial Work*, Harper & Row, 1973.
3. Stewart, R., *Contrasts in Management*, McGraw-Hill, 1976.
4. Mintzberg, H. 'Structured observation as a method to study managerial work', *Journal of Management Studies*, **7**, No. 1, February 1970.
5. Mintzberg, H., 'The manager's job—folklore and fact', *Harvard Business Review*, July/August 1975.
6. Mumford, A. C., 'Obtaining data on management effectiveness', *Journal of European Industrial Training*, **1**, No. 4, 1977.
7. Goffman, E., *The Presentation of Self in Everyday Life*, Penguin, 1971.
8. Goffman, E., *Encounters*, Penguin, 1972.

3. The effective manager and his learning needs

How do I find out if I need to learn?

Readers may know the saying: 'Some are born great, some achieve greatness and others have greatness thrust upon them'. It is my experience that this could be applied to learning needs which, too often, are thrust upon an unaware and probably unwilling manager. The approach I will take in this chapter is I hope predictable from what I have said in the first two chapters. If the manager operates in a highly individual way in a complex environment, then his learning needs are likely to contain many characteristics unique to him. Attempts to generalize managerial needs not only relate more to idealized concepts of the manager's job, as discussed in the previous chapter, but too frequently miss the real nature of the individual's personal situation even where the analysis is based on questions about skill requirements such as 'decision making' or 'communication—oral'.

There are necessities and virtues which apply to either extreme, individual or general, but I will start with the process which I consider most relevant, and which I think managers are less likely to see as the intrusion of an alien discipline. I start, therefore, with the reality of what a manager does, instead of with a statement of skills he might need. The issue, then, is first not a 'learning needs analysis' but a review of job objectives and requirements from which learning needs may later be drawn. This basic approach is more appropriate for defining needs for the current job than for deciding what is needed for a later job, and I pick up this point much later in the chapter.

Analysing needs—or selling products?

The vast majority of off-the-job management training, and a great deal of on-the-job development, is provided without such analysis, to the apparent satisfaction of client (boss), customer (manager), and supplier (management educator/trainer/developer). For a variety of reasons, some of them valid, it is often actually difficult for the suppliers to undertake the kind of approach I advocate in this chapter. The result is that much management training and development is provided in highly generalized form, partly because the suppliers lack the will to make it specific, and partly because the economics of the resource seem to make it necessary. It is in the interests of suppliers to concentrate on apparent similarities of job, and on similar elements within jobs. As a supplier, I know the reasons for this, but as client and customer I am annoyed by it, and even more annoyed by the failure of many courses to recognize the fact and deal with the problems involved. If the only economical answer in much management training is to provide general learning experiences rather than learning directly related to the individual, then attention and time should be given to the problems of transferring the learning to the real job situation (and indeed to the possibility of the offered learning experience actually being irrelevant).

Unfortunately, such provision is, in my experience and from my reading, extremely rare. Managers may, for example, be exposed to a learning experience on decision making. This is almost certainly based initially on incorrect suppositions about what managers do. An increasing volume of evidence supports my own somewhat surprised conclusion from observing managers in action; decision making, as a discrete process, is not present in many managers' jobs in either the volume or the oppressive finality which would be presumed from the literature. Even where it does exist, the nature of the decisions to be made and the context in which they are made vary so widely as to make general sessions on decision making of doubtful appropriateness. It may be that a common process can be defined which deals with both the prolonged decision making involved in locating a third London airport and the short-term decision making involved for the captain of a Jumbo jet approaching a rogue aeroplane in his space over Heathrow. It seems to me doubtful that individual learning needs will have been met without the two people concerned having been given a link between a well defined process and the specific demands of the situation they actually face. It is at this point that much of the breakdown between what is learned and what is applied occurs, and it is a breakdown which can be traced back to inefficiencies and evasive thinking at the stage of analysing managerial learning ideas.

I have chosen decision making as an illustration because it brings out again the issue of what managers do, as compared with what they are commonly supposed to do ('managers make decisions') and also because it highlights again how much difference can be concealed even within a modified generalization ('some managers make decisions, but the content and context vary widely'). Even more important in this chapter is the point that managers themselves need to be much more critical in their appraisal of the relevance of a learning activity to their own needs. There can be few managerial elements with greater face validity in a training programme than decision making. Yet for many managers there would be other elements which would be both objectively and personally more important. We have to find some better way of ensuring that people do not learn to do the wrong things well; we have, therefore, to define what the right things are.

Situational effectiveness

Relevant learning needs can most sensibly be drawn from analysis of what a manager needs to be able to do effectively. It will be clear from the review in the last chapter that, just as there is no single statement of what a manager's job consists of, there is no useful single list of elements of the job in which he should be effective, and no simple list of standards which can be applied to assess effectiveness in carrying out the manager's job. There is no universally applicable statement of effectiveness at a level which would be helpful to a manager who wishes to find out whether, or how much, he needs to learn. As I have shown, the required content of a manager's job is so contingent on the particular situation in which he is operating that precise and relevant statements of what he needs to be able to do well can only be drawn up properly by careful study of the objective requirements of the job and of the environment in which a manager operates.

The work of Valerie and Andrew Stewart[1] is among the most recent in confirming this view. They found that effective managers in a number of organizations shared some characteristics—for example, managing themselves in a productive way, communicating and thinking clearly—but that only one third of their effectiveness characteristics were common across firms and job levels. Since, in my view, there would also be some significant differences in the actual behaviour requirement in different situations even where there was a shared characteristic, the need for accurate statements about particular jobs rather than general statements seems to me to be further supported.

Defining effectiveness

From the point of view of defining learning needs, the concept of effectiveness is somewhat elusive, but essential. As I will show later on, attempts to get at learning needs directly are fundamentally inappropriate. Valid learning needs can best be derived from what the manager is supposed to be able to do effectively. I am not attracted to any of the definitions I have found in the literature. Campbell *et al.* offer what emerges as a parody of an academic definition:

> We define effective managerial job behaviour as any set of managerial actions believed to be optimal for identifying assimilating and utilizing both internal and external resources toward sustaining over the long term the functioning of the organization unit for which a manager has some degree of responsibility.[2]

Reddin's version does, however, bring out a crucial aspect:

> There is only one realistic and unambiguous definition of managerial effectiveness. Effectiveness is the extent to which a manager achieves the output requirements of his position . . .[3]

The worst feature of the way some managers do their jobs is that they confuse activity, what they put into their work process, with desired results. Activity is a seductive occupation for too many managers, who have no clear sense of purpose and direction, but like chickens with their heads cut off still manage to run around. Reddin's emphasis on 'output' is therefore useful. He describes elsewhere in the book the crucial difference between efficiency and effectiveness. Missing from this definition, however, is the crucial dimension of whether the results have been secured in the most appropriate way; the managerial equivalent of a sledgehammer cracking a nut meets his definition of effectiveness—the nut cracks. In my view, an appropriate statement at the level of generalization is that effectiveness has the following dimensions:

- Required task standards
- Level of achievement against those standards
- Effort expended in achieving standards.

To determine his current learning needs, a manager must look at each of these in the context of his job.

Task standards

Management by Objectives, the big wave of the 'sixties, crashed on the beach and, like most waves, seems to have left the beach much as it was before. While there are many more organizations who have experimented with MbO than there are organizations who have continued with it, it seems to me that in fact it has had a significant impact. The impact has, however, been more at the level of an awareness of the value of attempting to define priorities and desired results at a commonsense level than at the rigorous and highly structured level required by formal MbO systems. MbO is an attempt to force managers into a highly disciplined, rational approach to setting objectives and standards, and its failure is predictable from that statement, since there are not many managers who either want or are able to employ a highly disciplined, rational approach. Even in its later improved versions, such as Reddin's, the pain of the process is frequently not seen as justified by any improvements in output. Too often, arguments over the precise meaning of words replaces the valid distinction between an activity and a result. Again, with due respect to later versions, MbO had the virtue of concentrating attention on the individual manager's unique contribution, but had the accompanying defect of failing to give emphasis to the contribution of others.

The full MbO route to defining standards has, in my experience in industry and the civil service, proved to be too much against the grain of managerial behaviour and to require too much maintenance to be applied usefully with many managers. The initial process can be illuminating and productive in clarifying problems and issues, yet I have recently felt increasingly that these useful results could be produced without setting up an MbO system. Certainly, this is true for identifying learning needs; the MbO approach is too remote for any sensible manager to consider introducing it for that purpose. In those firms where it exists, however, it could be the basis of analysing needs, since for each objective or target, the manager can be asked, or ask himself, what he needs to be able to do skilfully, or know well, in order to achieve the desired results.

Standards and achievement

In order to get at learning needs, I recommend for most managers a simpler approach, which combines much of the essence of MbO with the practicality of the manager's real world and motivations.

1. What is the purpose of my job?
2. What standards are currently used to assess my performance, e.g.:
   - Financial measures
   - Production measures
   - Customer measures.
3. What standards ought to be used to assess my performance, e.g.:
   - Satisfaction of boss
   - Relationship with colleagues
   - Innovation.
4. What are the crucial aspects of effectiveness in my job, e.g.:
   - Technical knowledge (of product, profession, product being managed)
   - Managerial work
     —Defining own job
     —Handling information
     —Problem solving
     —Innovation
     —Managing time
     —Keeping things going
     —Looking managerial
   - Managerial relationships
     —Defining work for others (subordinates)
     —Agreeing work with others (colleagues)
     —Negotiating with others (customers, colleagues, subordinates)
     —Handling ambiguous organizational relationships
     —Using power and influence.

I should emphasize that this is not a complete list of possible areas of effectiveness, but a list of aspects which I have found most frequently. The list can be drawn up from scratch or from the document which most managers have somewhere, their job description. This latter document is, however, at best only a starting point, because most job descriptions specify activities rather than desired results, and tend to be inflated by political ambition or expurgated by political sensitivity.

Job descriptions are useful documents as what they are—maps indicating territorial boundaries and major routes—but they are not a good working base for identifying learning needs.[4] For this purpose the manager needs something which is three-dimensional rather than flat, that tells him the level at which he is achieving rather than the range over which he is putting things in.

Effort expended in achieving standards

The manager uses resources to get results—both from himself and from the people under his direct command. The effective manager makes the right choice about whose efforts are actually used and how far the expenditure of effort is taken. The ineffective manager tends to overuse himself, and to cause his subordinates to expend more energy in relation to a given task than either the importance of the task or the significance of the result justify. Much of the temptation to do this arises from an inability to think in terms of significant results instead of activities, and also from an over-emphasis on creating the right image. Thus, subordinates find themselves forced into spending hours producing figures 'in case the boss wants to know the detail behind that point'. I am not decrying the significance of knowing the important figures, but I am denying the relevance of some of the work that is done because it is too often done in a vacuum—masses of minute detail produced sometimes, it seems, in almost perverse denial of the need to concentrate on things which will contribute significantly to profitable results.

The effective manager, in contrast, balances the requirement for defensive political behaviour against the requirement for positive achievement. There are occasions when organizational politics demands superb performance through intensive effort on something which is essentially trivial. The effective manager tries to ensure that these are the exception rather than the rule, by monitoring how much of his managerial effort is going into these demonstrations, and, when appropriate, trying to adjust the conditions in favour of real performance. (Later in this chapter there are some illustrations of how a manager can choose what to do.)

Examples of effectiveness requirements

In order to substantiate my reasons for recommending a review of effectiveness areas as a precursor to defining learning needs, I will illustrate from some of the more unusual areas and leave some of the more familiar aspects for later discussion.

Defining own job

I have not actually encountered this as one of the criteria for managerial effectiveness in the literature, yet managers whom I and others have rated as effective generally have a clear picture of what their job is for and what they have to do in order to get their idea of the job accepted. The ineffective managers, in contrast, lacking a clear mental picture of their job, wander inconsistently over a range of activities and, as Saul Gellerman said, handle their subordinates' jobs heroically while nobody handles theirs.

In traditional methods of analysing learning needs, this element is unlikely to be revealed.

Looking managerial

I have referred in the previous chapter to the significance of how a manager perceives his role and how his performance in it is perceived by others. In a perfect world a manager would be judged on his achievements rather than on his portrayal of being a manager, according to objective standards rather than on indefinable qualities like 'credibility'. This is not in practice the case, and, indeed, judgements about managerial effectiveness continually confuse presentational and achievement aspects. Those making these judgements often feel rather guilty about expressing them overtly, and it is most unlikely that this aspect would be identified unless the effectiveness route is being followed. 'Looking managerial' will include, (in addition to the examples given in the previous chapter) speaking authoritatively at meetings, dressing as most managers do in the particular organization, getting into the office early (as distinct from starting work early).

Using power and influence

It is an extraordinary comment on the absence of real research on what managers do that there is so much guidance available on decision making and on motivation, and so little on the crude and subtle processes by which a manager exercises his power and influence within an organization. This is not a uniquely managerial skill, but it is certainly a make-or-break aspect of what the manager does. The ways in which a manager gets others to do things can be summarized as:

- Force: for example, a requirement that a proposal must be approved by manager X
- Positional authority: for example, since Y is a director, and X is not, Y carries more weight
- Knowledge: for example, 'the use of DCF in combination with ROI is the best answer'
- Reward: 'I strongly agree with what you have said; you might like to add one point . . .'
- Personal friendship: 'Jack, you know how important this project is to me . . .'

In the increasingly complex managerial world described in chapter 1, the effective manager is the one who can use these flexibly to meet changing demands. Beer and Davis put this point clearly in relation to learning needs:

> The integrator role requires a person to work with and through others. Such a person will probably have high needs for affiliation, moderately high needs for achievement and relatively low needs for power. He will have skills in leading groups in problem solving and decision making, communicating openly and effectively, and dealing with conflicts between people. In short the integrator must have the skills to manage others in accomplishing a task without the use of formal authority and power. His interpersonal skills, expertise, and personality must provide the leverage.[5]

The characteristic line manager's behaviour—strong, quick, and decisive—would be seen as dogmatic, closed minded, and bull headed if exhibited by a manager serving as an integrator.

Analysis and choice as a basis for learning

The great problem with even the analytical approaches to defining a manager's job (such as MbO or the version I have given above) is that, even though they encourage the question, '*Why* do you do that?' they still may provide the wrong basis because what the manager is doing is seen out of context. The 'effectiveness area' approach does help significantly to provide a control against the risk of helping the manager to do the wrong thing better, provided the question 'why?' is frequently employed. As I have shown, my approach also brings out areas not usually found through traditional approaches to identifying learning needs.

Another part of the context, however, still needs to be examined. We have seen that what a manager does is influenced by a wide variety of factors in the organization, and by his own perceptions of what his job should be. From the point of view of both effectiveness and learning, his perceptions may, however, be too limited. He may too readily accept conditions and conventions about what he does which are unnecessarily restrictive. While a sensible manager takes account of expectations of others, and of the culture in which he works, his perceptions about those expectations are quite often untested and potentially invalid. Until they have been tested, his effectiveness areas and consequential learning needs may be incomplete.

I was particularly struck by this in a consultancy project I did in one firm. The project was essentially concerned with how to improve the effectiveness of a group of managers, but it had some valuable insights into how limiting and self-fulfilling expectations about the behaviour of others can be. The managers were ineffective at least in part because they were unwilling to challenge the conditions creating their ineffectiveness. They could not learn how to be more effective without attacking those conditions, and they were initially very unwilling to attack the conditions—the way their boss behaved, the crucial relation-ship of their work to the future of the firm and the pressures arising from this. It was my job to help them to see that they had more options for behaviour than they thought they had, that they had more freedom to behave differently than they claimed they had. I did manage to help them both to recognize options and to learn to take them up.

At that time Rosemary Stewart had not published the book[6] in which she produced a model which I believe to be very important in helping managers to broaden their view of areas in which they should be effective and in which, therefore, they may have learning needs. She found that 'managers tend both to exaggerate the amount of choice that they have while failing to appreciate the nature of some of the choices that are available to them'. She uses three concepts:

- Demands: those task elements or task situations which are, to some extent, imposed on a manager by his boss, colleagues, subordinates, or customers
- Constraints: the limitations placed on a manager's power to act—for example, by organizational rules or by his boss
- Choices: the ability to select how and when to undertake a task, not responding simply to the pressures of demands and constraints.

The concept of choice is a major positive feature for the manager who wants to learn how to be more effective, because it assists him in the process of concentrating on those elements of the job which either he or the organization will most benefit from, instead of simply responding to the pressures of the hour.

It is possible to be rational and thoughtful as a manager, and not respond exclusively with a series of reflex jerks. I would extend Stewart's original suggestion about the effective manager by saying that he meets the legitimate demands of the job while exploiting the relevant choices which enable him to do it better. Both aspects may create learning needs for him.

Can a manager choose to be effective?

Although many of the differences in the way managers carry out their jobs are organizationally determined, it is observably the case that managers in similar jobs within the same organization, with the same boss, will give different emphases to meeting apparently the same effectiveness criteria. This can be explained as a matter of personal choice, arising either from the particular skills of the individuals concerned or from their psychological make-up, which causes them to seek certain satisfactions and avoid dissatisfactions. If the organiza-tional climate, the manager's boss, and his own predilections are all influencing what he does, it could be argued that his managerial life is determined, and that choosing to be effective in new directions requiring new skills is neither feasible nor desirable. While it is true that the opportunities to escape are limited, and that not all managers are capable of taking them, I have found encouraging evidence in my own work which shows that a number of managers can be released from their mental fetters about their jobs, and can be helped to cope with the need to learn to be effective in areas outside their current experience.

Appraisal and learning needs

It is logical to turn from effectiveness standards to appraisal, and it is, anyway, the most frequently used managerial approach to identifying individual learning needs. Appraisal, like many religions, is more frequently adhered to in principle than carried out effectively in practice. There are major difficulties in pursuing appraisal effectively as a means of defining performance achievements, collecting data for management resource planning, or establishing a level of merit for remuneration. The ineffectiveness of appraisal in these areas, however, frequently pales into insignificance in comparison with the low level of contribution to the identification of development needs often 'achieved' through appraisal. Perhaps because of a combination of emotional and intellectual exhaustion by the time this section is reached, perhaps because of a real lack of knowledge of learning opportunities (see chapter 6), appraisal is normally a blunt or misused tool for identifying learning needs. It has great potential, but the potential does not get translated into performance.

While, of course, appraisal schemes vary widely in objectives, methods, and presentation, some basic elements are very common:

- A review of the extent to which job objectives have been attained
- A review of the contribution made by certain managerial skills
- An opportunity to comment on personal characteristics which have helped or hindered effective performance
- A section on training and development needs or solutions.

The main direct contribution of appraisal to learning needs should occur from the last three elements; the first is a prerequisite for valid analysis but not a direct contributor. Unfortunately, as would be expected from what was set out in chapter 2, the managerial skills analysis is normally based on an inappropriate model. Thus, if managers are given any guidance at all, it may be suggested that they 'consider managerial skills such as planning, directing, motivating, controlling, communicating'. The Conference Board in the United States in its survey of appraisal practices found that:

> Only about one third of the firms conducted a job analysis of all positions to be appraised to ensure that factors measured or judged by the appraisal system truly related to the requirements of the jobs.[7]

I am astonished that their figure is so high. If learning needs are established through this route they are likely to be either highly generalized, or invalid, or both.

The personal characteristics element in appraisal is the focus of a lot of controversy, largely derived from the days when personal characteristics rather than achieved performance dominated appraisal. When MbO took over as the dominant theoretical base, it swept away consideration of personal skills such as leadership, decisiveness, acceptability to others, and (my favourite) integrity. These aspects have now been reintroduced in some schemes in order to take account of the fact that people who had splendid achievement records were somehow found to be unacceptable in other jobs. This return has been of no great help to identifying learning needs, since the personal qualities which are either given for assessment on the form, or which emerge unbidden from the boss, are extremely difficult to translate into solutions. With the exception of leadership, on which there are constantly arising innovative training courses which are further and further removed from managerial reality, appraisal of personal qualities tends to be a hopeless method of establishing learning needs.

Where appraisal includes a section on training (it is rarely called learning), it is usually directly related to the earlier sections: 'What training do you recommend to overcome the weaknesses indicated in Section 3?', with perhaps an additional reference to training for a future job. Given the opportunity offered by a specific request for training recommendations, the appraisal discussion ought to be a vibrant and exciting occasion for the learning manager, yet this is rarely the case. The reasons are imbedded in the nature of the appraisal process.

For our purposes in this chapter, it is necessary to be selective in looking at the problems of appraisal, and to concentrate on those aspects particularly pertinent to establishing learning needs. I do so in good conscience because helping flowers to bloom in a desert seems to me a valid endeavour, even though it means I am not tackling the problem of shrubs and trees (or indeed of why there is a desert).

The problems which affect learning, and which must be attacked by boss or subordinate and preferably both, are

- Clarity of objectives
- Appropriateness of style of participant behaviour.

Clarity of objectives

Many systems have several, conflicting, objectives. For appraisal to be a fully valid tool for identifying learning needs, boss and subordinate have to agree that this objective has primacy at least over resource planning or remuneration objectives. This is necessary because valid learning needs will only emerge from an honest review of performance against defined standards. If that honesty has to be fudged in order to meet other objectives (such as getting the right distribution of above-average performers in the department, or getting the right points rating for the next salary review), the learning needs identified will at best be those which it is organizationally safe to identify, not those which actually represent the real needs of the individual.

Management development advisers will not like this statement, because of the consequences of accepting it; see the last chapter for more advice on how to make their life more difficult, and the life of the manager more effective.

Style of participant behaviour

In this section I will be looking at those appraisal systems which require a discussion between boss and subordinate.

Appraisal has too often required managers and subordinates to behave in a quite uncharacteristic way once a year, with similar consequences to those brought about by bosses and secretaries engaging in unusual intimacies at the office Christmas party. Because of the normal mixture of objectives, the boss may be required to carry out any of the following roles:

—Boss: defining and redefining standards of performance
—Coach/helper: suggesting ways of improving performance
—Judge: awarding points or adjectives on performance
—Priest: listening to problems, and in some cases providing absolution
—Divine: defining future career possibilities.

In the process of carrying out the coach/helper role which is most relevant to establishing learning needs, the boss is required to:

• Establish rapport with his subordinate
• Maintain a listening rather than a talking role
• Act in a way suggesting that he is open minded on the issues under discussion
• Focus on the needs of his subordinate rather than on his needs for his subordinate to behave in a certain way
• Confront helpfully, rather than avoid or state negatively, sensitive issues
• Give appropriate and adequate feedback.

The subordinate, too, has an interlocking package of roles:

—Subordinate: the person whose achievements are being appraised
—Defender: offering explanations and exculpations
—Victim: holding the parcel when the music stops (how many appraisal forms contain a section on the contribution of the boss to failures?)
—Learner: defining areas for improvement.

In carrying out these roles effectively, the subordinate is required to:

• Assess how honest he can afford to be
• Ensure that the right data is reviewed (*right* meaning both accurate and relevant)

47

- Be sensitive to the needs of his boss
- Protect his own interests, as a person, as a manager with potential, and as a father with a mortgage
- Offer real knowledge of himself and his performance that only he can know
- Confront rather than avoid sensitive issues
- Seek appropriate and adequate feedback.

Clearly, the opportunities for both confusion and ineffective performance with incongruent roles and skills are considerable. Unfortunately, also, bad relationships built up on the performance elements of appraisal discussions, which usually come first, make a serious review of development needs additionally difficult. (A serious review is quite distinct from a ritualized review at a superficial level, which means that a subordinate is recommended for training from whatever catalogue of training events the organization happens to operate.) The appraisal discussion is a microcosm of the normal styles and skills of those involved in it, and of their expectations of each other. Normal behaviour patterns of dominance and submissiveness, of aggression and defensiveness, of emotion and rationality obtain. I have referred earlier in the book to the importance of the boss in a manager's learning environment, and will be looking at him again later. Some interesting ideas about boss/subordinate relationships in appraisal are given in a book by Lefton et al.,[8] which suggests why so little useful action emerges.

Managers and subordinates who do not expect to get much out of appraisal (and there are many of them) will certainly find their expectations fulfilled. Effective results will, however, come to managers and subordinates who really want to exchange views about themselves, their jobs, and their environment. A candid examination of standards, performance, and possible areas of improvement can be achieved, and from that achievement will come both a direct learning experience for both of them and also an identification of real learning needs.

Making effective use of appraisal

Clearly, I am pessimistic about the chances of really significant learning needs arising from many appraisal discussions, where the styles of either boss or subordinate or both, and conflicting objectives, are likely to prevent serious discussion. What, however, can be done to improve the use of appraisal for learning?

The boss should:

- Ensure that feedback is given in relation to defined standards, and is specific (because feedback which is general or not related to goals is frequently rejected)

- Assess the likely reaction of his subordinate to the appraisal discussion, and particularly to the further development part of it
- Assess the style which he himself is likely to use, and the impact of this on the discussion
- Calculate from these how deep the discussion of performance and development needs is likely to be. Is a discussion of 'which job next' and 'what about a course in chairmanship' the best that can be achieved, or can the discussion really take up issues of effectiveness?
- Discuss with his subordinate the possibility of agreeing development needs which are not recorded on the appraisal document.

The boss should do much more than this, but since this book is aimed at the other participant—the learner—it is appropriate to give more attention to what he should do. I will be dealing later in this chapter with the big issue of self-appraisal, but some aspects have already been mentioned, in the suggestions about defining effectiveness areas. These can be part of his contribution to the appraisal discussion, in providing the base from which desired improvements can be proposed. Where the subordinate is unfortunate enough to be the victim of an appraisal scheme which does not deal in objectives and achievements, he should propose them to his boss anyway 'as important background for what we are going to discuss'. I have been critical earlier about the kind of so-called managerial skills analysis, and of the personal characteristics which appear in many appraisals. These deficiencies can be turned to good account by the learning manager if he is prepared to do some work on translating the areas in which he is required to be more effective into performance characteristics, and to lead his boss into helping him define his performance on them.

An example may help to make this point. A manager giving a service at a very senior level found in discussion of his effectiveness areas that he had to be 'credible' with the senior people with whom he interacted occasionally. In appraisal it was said that he lacked credibility, not with his boss but with others, and this was derived from his contribution at meetings. In further discussion on what it meant to be 'credible', it became clear that what was at issue was not his technical competence but his ability to express that competence in a wider sphere at meetings. What had begun as a criticism ('You don't say enough and therefore lack credibility') became a performance requirement and learning need ('Acquire more knowledge of the nature of our business in order to contribute more and acquire credibility').

From a learning point of view, it is most useful for the manager to get away from generalized appraisal statements such as 'Needs to improve his planning ability', or 'His relationships with colleagues could be improved'. In discussion with his boss, the learning manager should, of course, seek to establish the validity of the criticism, by asking for it to be related to his required areas for effectiveness (thus avoiding the defensive/rejection syndrome). Then he should ask for specifics. 'What kind of planning, for what purpose?' 'What particular aspects of my behaviour towards which colleagues?' Real, rather than superficial, learning needs will emerge from an honest attempt to answer these questions, provided both boss and subordinate are prepared to accept the pain involved.

Harry Levinson[9] has given a number of illustrations from a slightly different perspective of why it is necessary to look at how managers achieve, as well as registering what they have achieved. From the point of view of the manager who wants to learn (but not to others), the *how* is the crucial issue. As Levinson puts it, 'he must be helped to differentiate the varied kinds of behaviour required to succeed'.

Self-appraisal

The idea of a manager appraising his own performance as an essential part of the formal appraisal process is written into many appraisal schemes. The powerful effect of self-identified problems, weaknesses, and solutions, as compared with exactly the same things identified and stated by the boss, is increasingly recognized. I have no doubt that this approach is more effective, both for appraisal overall and for establishing learning needs (where, indeed, the technique is frequently used even by bosses who otherwise do not request a contribution from their subordinates, because they can think of little to say). Many of the processes I have discussed in this chapter are a form of self-appraisal, although they may not be built into a formal process from the point of view of the appraisal system. Even where a manager is not required to appraise himself, I would recommend that one who wishes to learn does so, even though he may sensibly and legitimately be cautious about how much he reveals of his self-analysis.

While I think self-appraisal is a dynamic and potentially powerful element, it does bring out, if used in a formal appraisal system in a magnified form, all the basic problems of honesty, trust, and confidence inherent in the appraisal process. Again, these problems are too broad for discussion here. It is necessary only to say that it cannot be assumed that the potentially greater accuracy of learning needs identified through self-appraisal will actually be realized within the formal appraisal system.

Forms of self-appraisal outside the appraisal system bring in entirely different values, issues, and opportunities, and these approaches are covered in detail in chapter 8. One form of self-analysis—the way in which a manager spends his time—may, however, appropriately be dealt with now.

The use of time

It is at best paradoxical and at worst horrifying that most managers do not manage one of their basic assets, time. They tend to equate long hours and a feeling of exhaustion with effectiveness. There is no mystery about why they do not control the way they spend their time and do not allocate it in proportion to the real priorities and really productive aspects of their work. They do not control it because they do not measure how much time they spend on which activities, nor do they have standards by which they could assess whether their expenditure of effort is correct. Materials, labour, machines are controlled in this way, but rarely the manager's time. I met a manager a few years ago who was well known for the long hours he worked, for his attention to detail and for the fact that his subordinates could never get in to see him. He had no clock in his office, and had had two watches in a month which broke down. When I met him he mentioned this and then said: 'Would you believe I bought a third watch; it worked but I developed a rash on both wrists when I tried to wear it.' He was an extreme case, but he epitomized a common problem.

It is not my purpose in this chapter to add to the existing literature telling a manager how to manage his time in order to be more effective. I want to look at the ways in which the use of time can be measured from the point of view of how that measurement could contribute to establishing learning needs. Just as with the approach to learning needs through effectiveness areas, time analysis is a combination (preferably not an alternative) route to establish what the present level of performance is, the degree of satisfaction with that level of performance, and consequently the areas of knowledge or skill necessary to raise the level.

In common with many others, I have experimented with different methods of helping managers measure the way they spend their time. The approaches tend to be variants of the following main styles.

The chronological log

The advantage of this kind of log (see Fig. 3.1) is that it gives a very full and detailed statement, rather like a stream-of-consciousness novel. The disadvantage is that it requires a lot of subsequent analysis for meaningful interpretation to be possible. It can be a good document for discussion.

Readers might like to make a note of the issues they would choose to discuss with the manager concerned.

Again, readers should pause and see what they make of this information.

The activity log—Type A

The advantage of this kind of log (see Fig. 3.2) is that it gives you frequency and length of contacts, and at whose initiative they are made. The analysis is easy to do. It presumes some prior thought or discussion to establish that these selected issues are worth studying. The total at the bottom rarely adds up to the actual hours spent at the office; interruptions and panic situations get in the way of total dedication to the record.

Time	Activity	Comment
08.30	Reading mail	I like to start early
08.40	Telephone works manager on productivity report	I found the most important item down the pile
08.45	Reading mail	
08.55	Ask secretary to make 2 appointments arising from mail	Urgently needed to see works manager first, then production planner
09.00	Meeting with marketing and finance managers	Fall-off in sales affecting cash flow
10.10	Meeting with personnel manager	He wanted clarification on report he is writing for me today
10.20	Meeting with marketing and finance managers	Interruption did not help
10.30	Discussion with works manager	Productivity report
10.35	Telephone call from boss	What are you doing about this productivity report?
10:40	Discussion with works manager	Productivity report

Fig. 3.1. The chronological log

Time spent with

Person		Minutes	(Total)		His call	My call
Boss		5 + 10 + 5 + 5	25	~~IIII~~	4	0
Subordinate	A	65	65		0	1
	B	5 + 10 + 5 + 15 + 10	45		3	2
	C	15 + 25 + 5 + 5 + 5	55		4	1
	D	5 + 10 + 5 + 10 + 5	35		4	1
	E	25 + 5 + 5 + 5 + 5	45		1	4
Colleague	1	10 + 10 + 10	30		3	0
	2		0		0	0
	3	5 + 10 + 5 + 5	25		4	0
Secretary		15 + 5 + 20 + 5	45		0	4
Mixed meetings		120 + 65	185		2	0

Fig. 3.2. The activity log—Type A

There is a different type of activity log (see Fig. 3.3) which is also selective and based on some prior understanding of what is worth looking at. The analysis is easy to do. As with the previous log, it requires self-discipline to record the data. As one manager said to me plaintively, 'If I had that kind of self-discipline, I would not need a time log to tell me what is happening.'

Once more, readers might benefit from looking at these figures and deciding what they think is revealed.

Time span of activity		
5 minutes or less	~~1111~~ ~~1111~~ ~~1111~~ ~~1111~~ 111	23
6–29 minutes	~~1111~~ ~~1111~~ 1111	14
30–60 minutes	111	3
1–2 hours	1	1
Longer		0
Frequency of interruption		
Number of interruptions (i.e., someone else breaks into your work)		
Boss	11	2
Subordinates	~~1111~~ ~~1111~~ ~~1111~~	15
Colleagues	~~1111~~ 11	7

Fig. 3.3. The activity log—Type B

The point of time analysis

It is tempting to stay in the broad field of how the analysis of use of time can be used by a manager to improve his effectiveness. For present purposes, however, we are looking at the specific ways in which the time analysis can help a manager establish in which areas of his work he may have learning needs. For this purpose, the following questions can lead to useful issues:

1. How closely does the way in which I spend my time relate to the main objectives and priorities in my job?
2. On which tasks/issues should I have been spending less time?
3. On which tasks/issues should I have been spending more time?
4. Are there tasks/issues which I do not seem to be touching at all?
5. Who is in control of the way in which I spend my time?

I give now some examples of how learning needs could arise from answering these questions. (I emphasize that other needs may emerge as well—job clarification, organization structure, the relevance of some tasks.)

1. 'The first problem is that I have not sat down recently to determine what my objectives and priorities are; but I seem to spend most of my time fighting fires, which ought not to be a priority. The problem really is that it is not easy to work out what my objectives should be except in vague terms; how could I be helped on that?'
2. 'Like most managers, I should spend less time in meetings—my own and other people's. My meetings seem to get held up by interesting digressions, which I find difficult to stop. What should I do about that?'
3. 'From the figures (which surprised me), it could be argued that I should spend more time with some of my colleagues in other departments. The trouble is that they never seem interested to discuss things important to me. I go in with a subject and they manage to distract me. Is it me or is it them? Do I write them a formal memo or what?'
4. 'The analysis is an awful jolt. It shows that in two weeks I have had only one significant discussion with my finance manager. He sends me stacks of paper which I should discuss with him, but I don't understand most of it; I have never had to deal with financial figures before.'
5. 'Not me is the honest answer. When you come down to it, my subordinates seem to need to talk to me so much. There must be some reason why they can't get on by themselves; I seem to spend half my time giving them tasks and the other half sorting out the results with them.'

It may be useful to add one general point to the specific illustrations. Not surprisingly, managers tend to engage in those activities for which they are rewarded or from which they get satisfaction. One result from time analysis can be that it actually brings out for attention those things which a manager is *not* doing, which may turn out to be things from which he gets no satisfaction because he lacks skill or knowledge in those areas. This is why many managers find on undertaking this kind of analysis that they are spending time on an area of technical expertise rather than on areas of management. Thus I found the editor of a woman's magazine reverting to the fashion aspects, with which she was at home, rather than the production problems, which she knew little about; a technical director who was constantly veering back into the intricacies of the technology instead of managing the conflicting resource claims of his departments. Sales managers are notoriously likely to spend time selling rather than managing or helping others to sell.

Untraditional approaches to identifying learning needs

I have written for the situation which applies to most managers, who have to rely on existing management development systems and processes. The approaches have a common element in that they all depend on the participants' memory of what the behaviour of a particular manager was, and how effective it proved to be. Managers are not, however, used to the idea of logging behaviour, so the data is often both slim and the subject of argument. There is another approach to assessing individual needs which I have found fruitful, although relatively luxurious. I have observed a number of senior managers in operation and have been able to help them identify a number of actions which would help them perform effectively (one example is given on page 43). Observation of the kind I carried out has the great advantage of giving the possibility of observing specific behaviour and ways in which that could be changed; in learning needs terms, the issues identified ranged from how to structure and prepare for a weekly management meeting to analysing the particular kinds of contribution made at meetings.

Slightly less unusual is the use of an adviser to help managers establish their learning needs through an individual discussion outside the formal appraisal process. A few organizations have tried to eliminate the bad effect of appraisal on a development discussion by separating the two; in the normal boss—subordinate relationship the separation is not usually helpful. The use of an outside agent, however, offers more benefits; the reason for separating the discussion from appraisal is clear and workable; and the contribution of a professional development agent is frankly better than is usually achieved by most line managers. It is, however, again a relatively luxurious process.

Analysing common learning needs of managers

Quite a lot of effective work has been done to establish for coherent groups of managers what their learning needs are, first to establish the need for particular skills, and then to establish the specific forms of behaviour required for effective performance in that particular environment. I am thinking particularly about the original work[10] in British Airways and International Computers which led to the development of a whole new thrust on interactive skills training based on behaviour analysis. Rackham[11] has shown how this kind of approach can be extended into the area of negotiation skills, and Honey[12] has illustrated how managers can be helped to identify the difference between their stated behavioural objectives and their actual performance, and to see that they need to learn how to make these more congruent.

The repertory grid approach, although used as yet by relatively few management development people, is another way of identifying the actual behaviours required of an individual or a group of managers. A good illustration of how it can be used is given by the Stewarts.[13] The assessment centre approach to selection, based on a similar approach to defining behavioural characteristics, has potential for identifying learning needs, but is less frequently used for that purpose than for selection decisions.

There are other, more traditional approaches to identifying the needs of groups of managers, in which—usually by structured questionnaire—a trainer or management development adviser attempts to establish common features in jobs. The approaches vary between those based on some form of job analysis and those (more modern) which are based on a critical incident technique.

As I started this chapter by saying, these methods have their place. For groups of managers with similar jobs they may be the only effective and economical answer to defining learning needs and working out solutions to the needs.

For the purpose of this book, however, I have made the decision not to give a more detailed account of the processes, simply because the thrust of the book is to deal with the individual manager.

Colleague feedback and learning needs

I will be describing in later chapters various ways in which colleagues may be used as aids in learning, adding further detail to the indications I gave in chapter 1. Colleagues have no obvious role in establishing learning needs in the analytical sense (as distinct from providing a model from which a manager recognizes a need to learn). Feedback from a manager's boss is an essential part of the process of defining needs, and is sometimes actually explicitly geared to that process; feedback from a colleague normally differs in that it is not geared in the same way to identifying learning needs. The reasons for this are that it would be quite contrary to the normal organizational culture for colleagues to offer this kind of service, and therefore horrifying for most managers to contemplate receiving it. Therefore, except in a very few cases, a direct relationship between colleagues on identifying needs is not an acceptable proposition.

This should not mean, however, that a manager who wishes to learn can or should ignore the learning possibilities in feedback about his performance from his colleagues. Feedback is constantly provided unconsciously—i.e., not as feedback in a deliberate, controlled sense, but in the form of spoken and unspoken reactions to what a manager has done. The feedback can be consciously provided, perhaps at the direct invitation of a manager who wishes to know more about himself and his performance, and who is prepared to take risks in order to get this information.

Some examples of forms of colleague feedback, in which the learning implications are fairly clear are:

Case 1 Manager A attended a series of meetings with an important customer, accompanied by a colleague, B, from another department. After two meetings, his colleague came to him and suggested that there should be a change in the arrangement by which manager A made the initial presentation at the meetings: 'They clearly cannot follow the technical aspect of what you are saying; that is why they ask so many questions and the meetings aren't getting anywhere.'

Case 2 Manager X had acquired with a new department a subordinate, Y, fifteen years older than himself. He found himself constantly irritated by the propensity of Y to refer to the inviolate principles to which the department adhered, and the successes achieved through them. As a result, he recognized, he frequently challenged his subordinate and his views in an unproductive way. A colleague who attended these meetings commented casually to him over a drink, 'The long-lived fish is the one who doesn't always rise to the bait you know.'

Since the possible number of occasions on which feedback could be obtained from colleagues is enormous, the question obviously arises as to why it is in practice so little used. Why is the reservoir of information which we need to tap in order to find out more about ourselves left unused? Fritz Steele, in a book which gives a lot more helpful advice than I can find room for here, puts the reason clearly:

The short term costs of disclosure (embarrassment, loss of degrees of freedom, uncertainty) are experienced as more immediate and are therefore given more weight than are the long term gains of disclosure (true problem solving, learning from experience, etc.)[14]

Assessing needs for a future job

I have given most emphasis in this chapter to ways of finding out learning needs which are most clearly related to the manager in his current job. I am sure about the priority involved; too much development for future jobs has been built on very shaky foundations in the sense of what a manager has learned in and for his current job. The analysis of current needs could bring out aspects which are more related to a future than to a present job. The sharpness and specificity of analysis are, however, likely to be lacking, in the sense that neither the specification of performance requirements for a future (perhaps unknown) job can be done with similar effectiveness, nor can the manager's actual level of performance be tested fully in relation to the standards appropriate to another job.

The principles deployed in this chapter can nonetheless be maintained, so that learning needs for future jobs should be related to, at the least:

- Some attempt to define what sort of job and what sort of requirements he will have to meet
- Some attempt to define the level of skill, experience, or knowledge possessed by the manager, not against the requirements of his existing job but those of a future job.

It may be planned, for example, that a marketing manager should move next into a general manager job, although the specific job may not be known. What is his level of knowledge in the functional areas outside marketing? What has been his experience of managing older, and perhaps less 'intellectual', managers? Which areas of improvement required in his current job are likely to be even more important in his next job?

There is also a potentially big field of work in identifying future learning needs through analysis of future business needs as revealed in five-year plans, perhaps indicated by references to new technology, new products, new management techniques. In these cases, it is more difficult to use the effectiveness analysis approach I have recommended, but it is desirable to try and stimulate discussion on the ways in which requirements for effectiveness may change, and therefore the learning needs which may arise. The problem is likely to be that specificity is difficult to achieve, so that vagueness and generalization are the only things to emerge: 'Everyone will need to be marketing oriented.'

Clearly, many of the normal ways of identifying managerial learning needs are geared more to economy of effort than to accuracy and relevance to the individual manager. I have given in this chapter reasons why methods of analysis chosen and employed by the manager himself are likely to be more effective, considered simply as tools for needs analysis. Subsequent chapters will reinforce the point from the different perspective of identifying learning opportunities. If needs have not been properly identified by the manager himself, he is unlikely to spot learning opportunities related to them.

Questions

1. Do you think your current development is being managed on the basis of a thorough and systematic analysis of your learning needs?
2. Which of the processes described in this chapter could be used most appropriately in your own case?
3. Could the appraisal discussion as a means of identifying learning needs be improved in your case? What contribution could you make?
4. What aspects of the manager's performance indicating learning needs do you think are revealed in the time analyses given on pages 52 to 53.

References

1. Stewart, V. and A., *Managing the Manager's Growth*, Gower Press, 1978.
2. Campbell, J., M. Dunnette, E. Lawler and K. Weick, *Managerial Behaviour, Performance and Effectiveness*, McGraw-Hill, 1970.
3. Reddin, W. J., *Managerial Effectiveness*, McGraw-Hill, 1971.
4. Central Training Council, *Survey on Management Development*, HMSO, 1971.
5. Beer, M. and S. M. Davis, 'Creating a global organization', *Columbia Journal of World Business*, Summer 1976.
6. Stewart, R., *Contrasts in Management*, McGraw-Hill, 1976.

7. Conference Board, *Appraising Managerial Performance*, Conference Board, 1977.
8. Lefton, Buzzotta, Sherberg and Karraker, *Effective Motivation Through Performance Appraisal*, Wiley, 1977.
9. Levinson, H., 'Appraisal of what performance', *Harvard Business Review*, July 1976.
10. Honey, P., N. Rackham and M. Colbert, *Discovering Interactive Skills*, Wellens Publishing, 1971.
11. Rackham, N., 'The effective negotiator' *Journal of European Industrial Training*, **2**, No. 6, 1978.
12. Honey, P., *Face to Face*, IPM, 1977.
13. Stewart, A. and V., *Tomorrow's Men Today*, IPM, 1976.
14. Steele, F., *The Open Organization*, Addison Wesley, 1975.

4. Learning theories and the motivation to learn

My expectation is that many managers will have uttered a silent 'Ah yes,' in response to many of the points made in the first three chapters, because what I have written will chime with a lot of their own experience, and because I have given a number of concrete illustrations.

This chapter is a major contrast, and is much more risky because it attempts to describe theoretical issues in learning; many managers are not attracted by academic theories (while, of course, acting according to general principles of their own which they would not describe as theories). It is certainly the case that later chapters, while they do not depend on this one, will be better understood by some readers if they understand theories about learning. However, one of the points I will be making is that some people like to approach learning through first understanding abstract concepts (theories), while others approach learning more effectively through concrete experience. The chapter can therefore be experienced as a demonstration of one of the theories it describes. A reader who finds this process uninteresting and unhelpful could turn to subsequent chapters which contain little theory and many practical examples. On the other hand, reading this chapter will help him understand better why he prefers one kind of learning approach to another.

Understanding the basis of learning

There is no single universally accepted theory of learning. Even institutions whose business is to provide learning experiences seem to use, perhaps without conscious choice, several theories about learning. If there is no universally agreed definition, and no common application, the practising manager may wonder why he should attempt to concern himself with the theories. The reason is that understanding the theories may help him understand himself and his own learning processes better, and also help him assess the learning processes to which he is exposed by others. This could help him to be a more effective learner.

We need first a definition of learning. Managers will be familiar with the problems of definition, illustrated by the kind of experience often said to arise from a course. A manager may be said to have acquired new knowledge, but not be able to apply it. Some will argue he has learned something, others will argue that until he has been able to demonstrate what he has learned, it is impossible to say that he has learned. My own understanding is that it is sensible to say that a manager has learned if either or both of the following applies:

- He knows something he did not know earlier, and can show he knows it
- He is able to do something he was not able to do before.

The processes of learning are generally agreed to comprise four steps, with some disagreement on the descriptions and on degree of significance

Description	Explanation
Drive or motivation	What causes the wish to learn?
Cue or stimulus	What brings out the act of learning?
Response or act/thought	What action takes place?
Reward or reinforcement	What tells me the action was successful?

Most learning theories concentrate on the last three steps, in part because they are much more observable; it is very difficult to be sure what is actually causing the wish to learn. I will follow this pattern to the extent of leaving motivation for discussion after the theories describing the more concrete processes.

Before looking at the various theories of learning and illustrating the different contributions they make to our understanding I will describe those elements which seem to me common to all the main theories. The following seem to me to be the most relevant for managers:

- Reinforcement
- Reward
- Success and failure
- Knowledge of results
- Memory.

Reinforcement

The significance of reinforcement is illustrated in the example at the beginning of this chapter. Reinforcement can involve a repetition of the same learning process, or can be a further illustration of the desirability of the new learning. If a manager has learned a new technique for capital investment decisions, uses it on his return to work, and finds that it gives him a better basis for his decisions, his learning has been reinforced. If a newly acquired piece of knowledge or skill is not subsequently supported in the manager's environment, the new learning withers away or is positively extinguished.

Reward

Reward is a particular kind of reinforcement, but is an especially important part. The virtues of reward are that it not only reinforces the particular aspect learned, but also reduces the general feeling that learning is a risky business likely to lead to more disadvantages than advantages to the manager. Consciously or, perhaps more frequently, unconsciously, managers will undertake those learning activities which bring a prospect of reward rather than those which bring the risk of punishment.

Success or failure

Repeated success tends to raise the level of aspiration, whereas repeated failure tends to lower it. (The better MbO schemes are an example of the former.) Learning strategy, therefore, is best based on helping people to learn successfully, without eliminating the possibility of failure. However, since people are more inclined to examine the causes of failure than the causes of success, failure is not an entirely useless learning experience. The problem is that the analysis will only show what not to do, and failure is therefore, in a sense, a negative form of learning, not a way of building more effective behaviour; avoiding mistakes is useful but does not produce dynamic, innovative, effective managers.

Knowledge of results

The results of learning condition on-going behaviour; giving someone knowledge of the results of a newly learned form of behaviour is therefore crucial, since otherwise he will draw his own conclusions about the results. We know that:

- The information conveyed has to be specific, not general, because people cannot make much use of unspecific feedback. Thus, if a manager has been encouraged to learn more about investment appraisal, he needs to know that his boss recognizes his new skill on DCF, or believes that he still does not understand what counts as a capital asset.
- The information has to be conveyed in an appropriate way—which means in a way which is protective of the ego of the man who has learned, or not learned. There has to be real concern for the person receiving the information, otherwise resentment and hostility are likely to follow.

Memory

There is a basic problem of deciding at what time something has been learned. You cannot recall something that has not actually been absorbed. Accepting that something has been absorbed (i.e., a man can demonstrate learning at some stage), two reasons for the failure to remember something are particularly important. In general, the environment for the manager may discourage retention of learning if what has been learned is in conflict with the values or methods widely sustained in the environment in which the manager works (see chapter 1). The memory of what has been learned is wiped away because of the discomfort it causes. Similarly, if what a manager learns is in conflict with his own values, methods, or perceptions of himself, and the learning is in some sense superficial, the memory of the conflicting learning is erased.

Both environmental and individual explanations apply strongly on issues like managerial style, often the subject of learning on courses.

This subject brings out the fascinating problem of cognitive dissonance dealt with later in the chapter.

Different theories of learning

It is inconvenient that there is no single theory, and that different theorists give quite different weight even to the four basic stages in the learning process. Burgoyne and Stuart[1] have produced a list of 'Schools of thought on learning theory', any of which may be dominant, either explicitly or implicitly, in what is provided for the manager. Their list is:

- Conditioning
- Trait modification
- Information transfer
- Cybernetic
- Cognitive
- Experiential
- Social influence
- Pragmatic.

I have chosen to concentrate on three theories, which I believe to have been the most influential in shaping formally designed learning experiences, and yet also the most relevant to managers in helping them understand the way in which they learn on the job.

Behavioural learning theory

I prefer to use the term 'behavioural' rather than 'conditioning', as a more appropriate and less frightening adjective. The main theorist is B. F. Skinner.[2] His basic principle is that 'behaviour is determined by its consequences'. The immediate puzzle of how an act can be determined by something that happens after it occurs can be explained in two ways. First, much behaviour is undertaken in the expectation of certain consequences. Second, behaviour is undertaken in the awareness of the consequences which followed from the last occasion on which that particular act was performed. Skinner's argument is that the way to change behaviour is to change the consequences. Skinner is often quoted in a melange of 'behaviourists' or 'conditioners', so that he has become associated with Pavlov and bell ringing, brainwashing in Korea, and pulling habits out of rats, alongside a variety of disreputable and vaguely unethical activities.

The offensive element in Skinner, to many people, is that he says that man does not control his actions, rather that the actions are controlled by conditions created by general circumstances or manipulated by another person. Since, on the whole, people prefer to believe that they control most of their own actions, Skinner's argument is distasteful and unacceptable to them.

The argument that what people do is determined not by the process described by Skinner, but by a process internal to the person is clearly much more warming to the soul. This view is the antithesis of Skinner, not only because it takes the opposite view on what causes actions, but because, whereas Skinner deals in what is measurable (specific acts of behaviour representing consequences), the 'inner person' view deals with aspects which are often unmeasurable—and even, perhaps, unknowable. Alternatively, the opposition to the Skinner view emphasizes the presence of rational, calculating choice as a cause of behaviour.

Skinnerian theory gives exclusive emphasis to behaviour rather than thinking processes, and its exclusivity makes it a dangerous guide. It seems to me crucial that managers recognize how significant consequences can be, both in bringing about new behaviour (learning) and in extinguishing old forms of behaviour. A large part of this book has been concerned with explaining the environment which encourages or discourages learning, and provides the circumstances in which the consequence of behaviour (learning) is reward or punishment. However, to accept that many things essential to effective learning are wrapped up in the concept 'consequences' is not to accept that all things essential to effective learning are included in 'consequences'. One does not have to retreat to the mystic world of the soul or the unreal world of a totally rational calculating man to deny that learning man simply stands around waiting for consequences to happen to him, making no personal positive contribution. (I will therefore be taking the whole issue of the impact of personal motivation later.)

We do not have to accept the extreme Skinnerian form of behaviour and consequences to see that his theoretical 'school' has had a deep influence on our understanding of learning. I believe there are six major aspects of their work which should influence what the manager seeks in learning, and increase his understanding of what he is getting.

The first point is knowing what the consequences of particular items of behaviour are; the fact is that a great deal of managerial behaviour is undertaken with at best unclear objectives, and with little attempt to find out how far the consequences relate to the objectives. The result can be a form of learning which is positively disadvantageous to effective management, that a manager 'learns' from his understanding of the consequences a relationship between

64

action and result which is in fact incorrect. Thus, a manager who behaves aggressively in a particular situation, bringing about consequences which he likes, may learn that aggressiveness pays, without recognizing other negative consequences, less immediate or less relevant to him.

The second point is that Skinner is right to say that consequences can be managed—i.e., that particular consequences can be designed and built into an activity. In learning, consequences can be built which reinforce the desired behaviour, which reward it, and which increase the chance of the desired behaviour recurring. The reward can be material or psychological. It is, of course, also possible to use punishment (aversive consequences) in order to deter someone from using undesired forms of behaviour. As an illustration of these two processes in managerial learning, one can think of the managers who, having learned through a course how to delegate more effectively, find that the job is in fact done well, and that they have time to do other things. They have received a reward; if, however, their boss criticizes them for not knowing what is going on, they will have been punished for learning. I have talked of 'use', because it is possible to design situations in this way; it is equally important to recognize that much learning is uncontrolled, with rewards and punishments being distributed without any understanding of their impact on what people learn.

The third point is that learning does not remain effective unless it is reinforced; if the consequences of learning in the sense of changed behaviour, are that nothing happens, the newly learned behaviour is extinguished. This is particularly important in terms of the timing of reinforcement; reward that is distant from the event, such as a future promotion, may not be an effective reinforcement.

The fourth point is that the 'consequences' theory gives us a better understanding of the common phenomenon of people becoming less effective in using a skill unless they continue to practise it. This has usually been explained in terms of people forgetting the elements of the skill, by analogy from the physical or 'motor' skills; in managerial learning it is probably more relevant to think in terms of the absence of reinforcement leading to a return to the situation before the learning occurred.

The fifth point is that the consequences theory reminds us of the power of the environment in which a manager learns, and in which he applies his learning. Whereas the first four points are particular to an individual manager and his situation, it is useful to see him in the wider context in which he operates, and which rewards or punishes him for his behaviour, as we saw in chapter 1.

The final point is that the theory not only concentrates on actual behaviour rather than on beliefs about what causes the behaviour, but it attempts to help people learn by giving them quantified data about their behaviour. This has a direct relationship with many of the more modern approaches to improving interpersonal behaviour, in which managerial behaviour is split into categories such as building, supporting, proposing, which can lead to an analysis of the consequences of these forms of behaviour.

It may be thought that much of the argument about exactly what weight should be given to demonstrated behaviour (i.e., consequences) as a force in learning becomes confusing. The main point seems to me to be that a great deal of learning theory has over-emphasized the cognitive or inner state elements, and that the behaviourist theory has equally over-emphasized the measurement and control of behaviour. This imbalance is seen sadly in an otherwise fascinating book by Luthans and Kreitner,[3] explicitly based on the premise that 'behaviour is a function of its consequences'. To the contingency and data elements mentioned above, as two of their fundamental principles, they add as a third the necessity of dealing *exclusively* (my italics) with observable behavioural events. As I will show now, by looking at some other learning theories, I am unable to accept the word exclusively even in relation to the behavioural aspects of learning.

Experiential learning theory

Behavioural learning theory has been developed alongside another explanation of learning with which it would seem to have a lot in common. This is the experiential school, with roots in laboratory training and T-groups. The common element, not usually recognized by the proponents of either theory, is that both give a considerable emphasis to the actual experiences through which people go as the starting-point for the learning process. Whereas, however, the behaviourist school concentrates on consequences and seeks to design learning in order that the consequences of behaviour are controlled, the experiential school gives more emphasis to analytical cognitive processes as crucial elements in learning. The experiential school, therefore, brings back the idea of thinking as an adjunct to behaviour. As we will see later, awareness of the different balance of approach in particular individuals between learning by doing and learning by thinking after doing is crucial for a manager's understanding of his own approach to learning.

It may be helpful at this point to emphasize that experiential learning theory is not simply a jargon description of something many managers would call (without applying the epithet 'theory') learning from experience. Nor is it, as some organization development practitioners suggest, simply another description of T-group experiences of learning about feelings, about 'self'. It is a total explanation of a variety of forms of learning experience.

The experiential learning model is important both as a general learning theory and as a means of explaining differences in individual learning style. The model describes a circular learning pattern in the way shown in Figure 4.1.

As described by Kolb and Fry,[4] learning change and growth are best facilitated by an integrated process that:

- Begins with here-and-now experience
- Is followed by collection of data and observations about that experience

- Continues with analysis of that data
- Reaches the final stage with modification of behaviour, and a choice of new experiences.

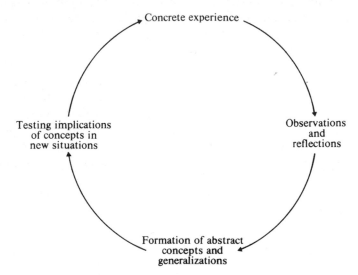

Fig. 4.1. A circular learning pattern

Experiential learning, although derived from the socio-emotional experiences encouraged in T-groups, adds the crucial cognitive element, the view that to be fully effective a learner has to use cognitive processes to make sense of the experiences in which he has engaged. The ability to be effective in all stages of the learning process seems, however, not to be widely shared, most particularly because the stages involve, in fact, different abilities, different styles of behaviour. Kolb and Fry conclude that individuals consistently prefer one learning style as against another. The detail of these styles will be described later; at this point the important issues for learning theory of the Kolb and Fry work are:

- The idea of a cycle of learning
- The concept of different individual approaches to learning within that cycle
- The emphasis on learning from a variety of experiences in life, not just from events designed for learning
- The understanding of the interaction between the process (the cycle), the individual (learning style), and the environment (which style is encouraged by task and content).

In my view, although not stated by them, another important aspect of modern learning theory can be derived. This is that the activity of learning is a skill which can be developed, not simply an activity responsive to a teacher or to an environment. Given the changes in learning needs which many managers will face, and the changes in the environment which influences their learning, an improved understanding of learning processes—and especially of what is meant by learning from experience—is crucial to the learning manager. Successful experience can indicate the right course of action when you are working in the same conditions in which you were successful, but many managers find that the conditions are not, in fact, quite the same. Simple repetition of past experience is often ineffective; learning needs to be seen as a much more considered process. The Kolb/Fry theory offers to managers the possibility of learning how to learn from new experiences quickly and effectively, in situations in which the gradual build-up of prolonged experience may be neither available nor acceptable. Perhaps even more important, experiential learning theory helps to explain why experience is not by itself a very efficient learning process. Managers are characteristically more concerned with succeeding, achieving results, winning, than they are with the process by which they succeed, achieve, or win—and knowing why they have succeeded may be the real learning need.

Cognitive learning theory

C. B. Handy[5] gives an explanation of learning which seems to me to illustrate a basically cognitive approach, one which emphasizes internal mental processes. He talks of the following processes in learning.

Exploration

The individual asks himself: 'Is there a problem?' 'What do I need to know in order to be able to deal with it?' When the problem is internalized (i.e., understood and accepted through the man's own thinking processes), real learning can follow, as compared with temporary learning when a need is 'forced' on the manager and not internalized.

Conceptualization

The individual sets a particular experience into a more general context, and makes some kind of general statement, which is a concept. In Handy's view, 'Without concepts, the isolated experience becomes mere anecdote, an experience talked of but not learned from'.

Experimentation

As a result of forming a concept, the individual takes action consistent with the concept he has formed.

Consolidation

Concepts are internalized and begin to mesh. The concept ceases to be tentative, and habitual behaviour is altered to fit the concept. The lesson has been learned.

There may seem to be considerable similarities between this and the Kolb theory; the difference seems to me to be the crucial one that Handy insists on the primacy of 'concepts' in learning, a primacy apparently unqualified by reference to different learning styles. The emphasis is, in my view, more flattering to the idea of thinking managers than an accurate reflection of how many managers learn.

Is there one correct learning theory?

Disraeli, speaking at a time when the Darwinian theory of evolution had shocked Victorians, said there was some dispute as to whether man was descended from apes or angels; 'I am on the side of the angels'. My own position on the various theories described here is that I see no need to choose between them. The experiential school—with its emphasis on the involvement of the whole person, of man as an emotional being, of his right to choose the kind of learning process he will experience, his right to be an adult not an overgrown child—seems to me very relevant. The cognitive school—emphasizing learning through contructed problems, through reflection and careful analysis of experience, giving weight to intellectual and rational processing—seems to me equally significant. The behaviourist school—with its emphasis on the influence of the environment, and its insistence on dealing with behaviour rather than attitudes—seems to be entirely right for those areas of learning which are essentially about interpersonal behaviour.

I believe the theories deal with different aspects of learning, and have different values for different learning needs, which may relate to different people or to different stages of development in the same person.

The motivation to learn

As I showed in chapter 1, there are a number of influences in the environment of the manager which help to determine his attitude to learning. Although this section deals specifically with the internal motivation of the learning manager, it is important to remember at the outset that this motivation does not exist in isolation from external influences, but is a factor constantly interacting with or against those external influences, expressed as consequences for what he does. As we shall see, motivation is difficult to describe, and difficult to assess in an individual. How people behave as learners is the important thing, but we may be able to help with behaviour better if we look at motivation as well.

A general motivation to learn?

It seems to me sensible to separate two strands in the motivation to learn. One strand is the general motivational make-up of the individual manager, those psychological elements which cause him to want to improve, change, and develop. The other strand, to which I return later, is the specific motivations which may apply in relation to particular issues on which a manager may have a learning need.

The first problem is to define what we mean by motivation, and the first hurdle to overcome is to replace the understanding which many managers have of motivation. (Since this new learning clashes with old learning, we are incidentally illustrating one of the problems mentioned earlier in this chapter.) For many managers, motivation is something which you pump into others—'to motivate' appears in some of those lists of managerial activities which I mentioned in chapter 2. Motivation is in fact something intrinsic to a person, not the result of someone else's manipulation. Intrinsic motivations can be encouraged or discouraged, but a manager cannot be motivated to learn by someone else, or by some external event; these can only release a motivation to learn which the manager already has. (Some writers do distinguish a category they call *extrinsic motivators*, of which financial reward or status are illustrations. I am not convinced by the distinction and therefore have not used it.)

Motivation is a psychological process which causes an action; it is based on, but is not the same as, a psychological need. This can be illustrated for our purposes by taking a psychological need found in many managers and showing how it may lead to motivation to learn.

Many managers have been found to have a high need for achievement. Their managerial activities are related to that need—they do things in order to satisfy the need, and what they do or do not do is influenced by the perceived or felt relationship between the activity and the need. If a manager sees no connection between his need and his activity, he does not undertake the activity. Motivation is the connection. A manager is not caused to take a particular action by his basic need for achievement; he may be motivated by his belief that the action will help to meet that need, which means he believes the consequences will be beneficial. This can be illustrated as follows:

- A manager may have a strong need for achievement
- He may expect that if he participates truthfully in an appraisal, barriers to improved achievement will be identified
- He may believe that if the barriers are identified, he will achieve more.

His motivation is the combination of the last two elements.

It can be seen that two managers with the same kind of psychological need could be motivated quite differently, and therefore act differently, depending on their beliefs about the relationship between an action and their needs.

The relationship has been expressed in more theoretical terms in Handy's general motivation calculus,[5] which is based on expectancy theory:

(a) The strength or *salience* of the need

(b) The *expectancy* that effort will lead to a particular result

(c) The *instrumentality* of that result in reducing the need in (a).

I have chosen to illustrate the progress between need–motivation–action from the need to achieve because it is likely to be a strong cause of motivation to improve performance, and if learning is seen as closely related to improved performance the motivation to learn will also be strong.

As with learning theory, there is no agreement yet on either a general theory of motivation or on the application of motivation theory. A great deal of the theory behind manager development in the 'sixties was built on the theories of three Americans; in addition, no respectable management course was complete without a session giving obeisance to their theories. Maslow's *hierarchy of needs*, Herzberg's *motivation/hygiene theory*, and McGregor's *Theory X* and *Theory Y* became part of the vocabulary of the well educated manager. I saw them myself as extremely powerful and hopeful explanations of needs which would motivate managers to develop and learn. Guest,[6] however, has shown that these theories have not been substantiated, and favours instead the work of Alderfer. Two elements in Alderfer's work seem to me important for learning. First, he talks of growth needs, the desire to be creative and to achieve full potential in the existing environment. Second, he distinguishes between needs which persist over time (to which he gives the unfortunate title 'chronic'), and needs which are situational and can alter with the environment ('episodic').

Causes of the motivation to learn

I have identified from my experience five major types of motivation to learn; they should be useful to a manager who wants to assess his own motivation.

Recognition of need

Some managers are motivated as a result of recognizing that there are areas in which their current performance could be improved, or areas of skill or experience which are less than they need to be for a future job. The motivation to learn may in these cases be wrapped up with issues of self-esteem, job security, status, recognition by peers—that is, basic needs which, when threatened, are transformed into a motivation to learn.

Success model

Even without a recognition of their own performance as being in an absolute sense 'weak', some managers recognize the greater skills of others, as demonstrated by their success, and decide to try and perform in the same way.

71

Failure model

The harsh facts of industrial life produce managers who fail, who are sacked, or who are placed in a backwater; in those cases where a lack of skills or experience is perceived as contributing to the failure, some managers decide to try to avoid a similar fate by acquiring skills or experience themselves.

Desire to improve

In contrast to those who are motivated by a sense of relative weakness in some area, some managers feel themselves to be effective, highly skilled, or possessed of the appropriate range of experience, and yet strive to improve themselves further either by adding new skills or building on their existing base. There seem to be two kinds of motivation involved: one a desire to sustain a reputation as the best, the other a desire to achieve a higher level of perfection.

Desire to compete

Some managers have strong drive to do better than someone else, or not to be at a disadvantage with experts. Since competition is in general a strong feature of managerial lives, it is not surprising that it can be present in learning motivation. An American manager who took an MBA by evening study told me he did it because he 'didn't want to be intimidated by marketing and finance people'.

Coping with insecurity and risk

Clearly, there are strong motivators which may bring a manager to the brink of learning. Equally, there are strong motivators which may lead away from learning. The most powerful derive from the need to avoid insecurity and risk. These two factors arise at both major stages of the learning process, the identification of needs and acceptance and incorporation of a learning experience. At the learning needs stage, managers are faced with the problem that to the extent that they agree learning needs they are accepting a lower valuation of their managerial performance, with the risk that this lower valuation will affect current status, and confidence of others and future promotion as well. At the stage of the learning experience itself—particularly if the learning experience is the major feature of the activity (and not a subsidiary part of another business activity)—the manager faces the problem of entering a new field, of risking his concept of himself as a successful manager in a new situation outside his control. If he continues in his previous mode, he controls the situation in terms of his past experience, and exercises those skills with which he is familiar and relatively successful. In a learning experience, he takes the risk of experimenting with new forms of knowledge and new skills, with the risk that not only will he not be able to apply them but that he will be seen to be unable to apply them—with risks for his acceptability both in his current job and for future promotion.

Some managers are better able to cope with these risks than other managers are. They may lack the level of introspection and self-doubt which would inhibit some managers from taking the risk, or they may respond on balance more to other motivational urges which pull them into learning situations despite the risks involved. One of the contradictory aspects of courses as learning experiences is that while in some respects they magnify risk by requiring course members to show knowledge or skill, they may reduce risk by making everyone seem unskilled or ignorant, or by providing a 'stranger' environment in which a manager is not exposed to his colleagues. The fear of failure may be a stronger inhibitor of learning than the fact of failure.

Again, we have to relate the actual expression of motivation to the context in which it occurs. If the environment for the manager encourages personal innovation, risk taking, and adventure, risk and insecurity will not be such powerful demotivators for learning. The trick for the manager is to recognize whether he is in such an encouraging environment.

Since motivation is intrinsic, the motivation to learn occurs initially and most strongly at the place of work, not at the place of learning. If a manager is not motivated to overcome his feelings of risk and insecurity in his work environment, it is unlikely that the learning environment will help him overcome them. Indeed, a basic problem of dealing with the motivations of an individual is that the motivations emerge as recognizable behaviours in a particular environment, and that individual behaviour can only be understood within that environment, in the dynamic inter-relationships which exist in a particular situation.

Cognitive dissonance

A great deal of the motivation to learn depends on the perceptions of the potential learner. How does he see himself, his level of performance? How does he see and interpret new experiences which, if understood and incorporated, become learning? If several people are involved in the same event, it is common experience that they will have different mental pictures of it, depending on their interests, level of involvement, perceptions of other people involved. A manager's picture of an event, and his capacity to learn from it, is affected particularly by the process of *cognitive dissonance* described by Festinger.[7] His theory is that when people find themselves in a situation in which two of their own strongly held beliefs are in conflict with each other, they find it difficult to cope with this internal conflict. They resolve it by adjusting one or other of their views, thereby reducing dissonance.

In learning terms this theory seems to me to help us to understand how some managers can dismiss a particular piece of knowledge or experience. It may not be simply that it does not fit their past knowledge or experience, but that it does not fit in a particularly uncomfortable way. If a manager has had success with a particular kind of behaviour, and then is exposed to an experience (probably a course) which exposes the negative consequences of that behaviour, he is most likely to reduce the dissonance by denying the validity of the second experience. 'Well I agree Jack got upset, but in real life . . .'

The Festinger article is particularly relevant to the processes of learning by association with others. It also has strong associations with the issue of stereotypes, since new information which conflicts with stereotypes creates dissonance. Thus someone who is racially prejudiced, who meets an intelligent black man will finds ways of denying his intelligence or qualifying his blackness. Whoever met a warm-hearted, impulsive accountant?

In learning situations, the impact of dissonance arises most strongly from feedback about behaviour. If a manager is told by his boss, a colleague, or a trainer that a piece of behaviour is inappropriate, whereas he had previously thought the behaviour to be correct, he may, as shown earlier, dismiss the point as arising from an untypical situation (a course). Dissonance is then at a low level. He may have a much more difficult situation, however, if the feedback comes from someone he respects, in a situation he believes to be more typical.

Dissonance also arises when managers are asked to look at an unsuccessful action of their own as part of a learning activity. Since failure is not a desirable managerial atttribute, recognition of your own personal contribution to it is dissonant with your desirable self-perception. The dissonance is managed either by decrying the importance of the activity ('Planning is a waste of time'), or denying the possibility of an effective contribution to it ('How can I spend time on planning when the unions are banging on my door every five minutes?').

Motivation in relation to specific learning opportunities

Handy's *motivation calculus* helps to provide a theoretical explanation of why someone who may well have basic motivations to learn in general, none the less does not have the motivation to learn from a particular learning activity. In this theory, the reason is that the prospective learner does not believe that the activity will really help to satisfy his need. Two perceptions are important here: the perception he has of what his need actually is, and his perception of the learning event. Both perceptions can be inaccurate, but motivation to learn will not be present unless the perceptions of need and provision are both positive. His perception of what his need is will be substantially affected by the process by which those needs have been established; a process which emphasizes uniqueness and reality in the way I have argued in the previous chapter is more likely to lead to a positive motivation towards learning in general. In relation to specific events, however, motivation can be either positive or negative in relation to the event, depending on its relevance to his recognition of his need.

The theoretical analysis is supported by everyday experience; managers fail to learn from apparently appropriate learning events for a variety of reasons, but one reason certainly is that they are not motivated for that particular event. Some demonstrate their lack of motivation by a bored disengagement, others by various forms of destructive behaviour. They may not have the motivation for this particular event at this particular time, or they may not believe in the validity of the kind of process involved ('I never learn anything from courses', 'How can you do a good job and analyse your learning processes as well?'). They may dislike a particular learning method within a course ('Business games are for kids', 'Lego bricks—how can I tell my colleagues I learned from building a tower?').

His general attitude to the particular kind of experience mentioned above is related to:

- His perception of the relevance of the particular experience to those learning needs which he has accepted as real to him
- His perceptions of the difficulty or risk involved to him in attempting to learn through that experience
- His beliefs about the rewards secured by others who have been through a similar learning experience
- His perception of the level of encouragement offered by his environment in general, and his boss and colleagues in particular
- His perception of the relation of the experience to the ways in which he believes he has learned in the past.

This latter point brings us into the area to which increasing attention is now being paid. Instead of seeing learning as, in a sense, a single, generalized process, we now see it more clearly as a process which applies differently to different people. Whereas ten years ago we talked of learning methods in a general sense as being more or less appropriate for managers, we now see that much of the previous argument over the appropriateness of case studies, or of discovery learning, or of action learning is quite beside the point. There is no uniquely appropriate method, because different managers have different styles of learning. Just as particular motivations are present more or less strongly in a manager, influencing more or less strongly his general motivation to learn and his specific interest in a particular learning experience, so there are different distributions within managers of what has been described as 'learning style'.

Managerial patterns of learning

I am indebted to some research by Dr Donald Markwell of Unilever for clarifying a useful point about the kind of learning which is most likely to engage a manager. He has pointed out that many 'academic' learning experiences start from an assumption of individual learning, often on a highly competitive basis, whereas managerial learning is much more social, the product of interaction, whether achieved on the job or on a course. He also has emphasized the extent to which much management learning is the product of experiment and self-discovery rather than of conceptualization and learning from a teacher.

The social learning issue is an important point to remember. In my anxiety to help identify the uniqueness of each manager and the special features of his learning needs, I have quite consciously omitted extensive discussion of generalized approaches to analysing his needs. I am a long way from saying, however, that it is possible for an individual to learn much on his own. In a later chapter I will be looking at how he can get colleagues and his boss to help him, but at this point it is necessary to emphasize how much learning (in the sense of changed behaviour) has to be seen as something dependent on the reactions and involvement of others. A managerial learner needs the help of others to understand what has happened, and he needs their encouragement and support if he is to incorporate his understanding into changed behaviour.

The group, or social, aspect of learning has, of course, strong resonance with the organization development approach, which emphasizes the need for understanding systems and for helping complete units to learn. This large and fascinating field is one which is relevant for context, but one which I have chosen not to give full emphasis to in this book since it is well covered in a plethora of OD literature.

The experiment and self-discovery point made by Markwell expresses a major concern which will be developed at greater length in the next chapter. How far is it possible to say that unless the manager is in charge of his own learning process, is a self-organized learner, he will not in fact learn? Some modern theorists seem to have adopted what is a possibility for some managers as a requirement for all. The idea of self-organized learning seems to me essentially concerned with the rational, thinking, or conceptual processes involved in learning—but these processes are by no means dominant, either in learning in total (see Kolb) or in individual managers, as we will now see.

Styles and skills of learning

R. W. Revans,[8] writing about the desirable content of management education, said that it should help managers acquire an awareness of the nature of their own learning processes: 'Indeed there is something to be said for the opinion that the first objective of management education is to acquaint the subject with this awareness.' The original Revans action learning programmes certainly did something to meet this objective, although not all its derivatives have done so.

Revans is explicitly saying that managers will benefit if they know more about how they learn; I take it to be implicit that by talking of 'their own

76

learning processes' he is also saying that different managers have different learning processes. There is a degree of conflict involved in accepting both propositions, since, as I will show, some managers are not happy with the cognitive processes of learning, and therefore would find it hard to think about their own processes. However, I accept both propositions as the starting-point for this section.

The general theories of learning reviewed earlier have dominated the field of knowledge about how people learn, so that only relatively recently has research begun to catch up with the common experience that different people learn most effectively in different ways. The best-known research is that of Kolb.[4] I have already used his general theory of the learning cycle (see page 67), but his special contribution is not, in fact, in describing this cycle (although it is frequently used) but in his attempt to analyse different learning styles. He takes the four stages of the learning cycle, which with slight changes of title become

- Concrete experience: learning from personal experience
- Reflective observation: observing, analysing, pondering about events
- Abstract conceptualization: constructing patterns of relationships
- Active experimentation: learning by 'having a go'.
  (The interpretations are mine rather than Kolb's)

Kolb claims that: 'As a result of our hereditary equipment, our particular past life experience and the demands of our present environment, most people develop learning styles that emphasize some learning abilities over others'. By the use of a questionnaire, the learning style inventory, Kolb measures an individual's relative emphasis on each of these four learning abilities. He has found that mangers tend to emphasize active experimentation over reflective observation. By further study he has established four statistically prevalent learning styles, where two of these abilities are combined as follows:

—The converger: combines abstract conceptualization and active experimentation (practical application of ideas)
—The diverger: combines concrete experience and reflective observation (generating ideas)
—The assimilator: combines abstract conceptualization and reflective observation (creating theories)
—The accommodator: combines concrete experience and active experimentation (carrying out plans).

The accommodator's learning style is said to be based on a general approach which consists of

- Doing things
- Carrying out plans and experiments
- Involving himself in new experiences
- Adapting himself to specific immediate circumstances
- Solving problems in an intuitive trial-and-error manner.

Unfortunately, although Kolb says that the converger is often found in engineering, the diverger in arts, and the assimilator in research and planning, he does not say where the accommodator is found; from the description above, I would expect many line managers to be among this group, and he suggests elsewhere that marketing people fit this category.

Kolb's research is relatively new and untested, and should not be accepted simply because it is the newest research of substance giving a theoretical basis for understanding likely managerial approaches to learning. The learning style inventory which he employs certainly needs wider validation before it could be proposed as a generally usable instrument. His research does, however, highlight certain points which check with my experience.

Concrete/abstract

The clash which he observes between these two abilities is borne out by my observation of managers. Most prefer concrete, specific experiences as a basis for action rather than abstract concepts. (They tend to use the term 'theory' only for the latter, and then as abuse.)

Active/reflective

I have earlier in the book given as my view that most managers are more active than analytical. If I qualify that to allow that many managers do attempt to plan activities, I would confirm the basic point, which is that most managers do not give significant time to reflecting on past experience; they use it, but do not analyse it. Most managers are profound believers that Hamlet could have done what was necessary much more quickly if he had not spent so much time thinking about it.

Courses as learning experiences

Business school courses, and many in-company imitations of them, give emphasis to concepts, analysis, and reflection rather than to action. These are distant both from the reality of managerial life and from the imbedded learning styles of many managers. This does not mean that such courses are unsuitable for managers, but that they may be more successful for some managers than others, and that we ought to be testing for selection more carefully.

Teachers and learners

The problem often stated—that business school teachers lack relevant experience and are unable to relate their theories to the practical needs of their students—may be insufficient; the probability is that such teachers also have a different view from their students about what learning actually involves. In the

academic world, concepts are important, and academia tends to attract conceptualizers, who naturally arrange learning for others according to their own
style, which is not the preferred style of many of those they teach.

Business school faculties are not the only teachers whose preferred learning
style may be in conflict with those that they are trying to teach. Equally, a
number of trainers outside business schools have adopted a theory of learning
which gives entire emphasis to providing concrete experiences, and encouraging experimentation. While this seems to match the preferred style of many line
managers, it does not meet the needs of those who wish to reflect or conceptualize.

Rigidity of learning styles

While I am not sure about the particular definitions applied by Kolb, I am clear
that many managers are attached to a particular learning style, and that their
attachment tends to be reinforced by the environment in which they work-
— 'Never use the word "theory" in this company'—and by the fact that successful and pleasant learning experiences tend to coincide with the preferred style,
while unsuccessful or unpleasant learning experiences are felt to be in conflict
with it.

The proposition that a learning style may be maintained strongly by one
person and criticized or found unhelpful by another seems to be substantiated
both in theory and in practice. Yet the theory also suggests that the really
effective learner would be effective at all stages of the Kolb cycle, and in all
main learning styles. Rather than allow any individual to retain a rigid treat-
ment of opportunities for learning, it would seem to be desirable and necessary
to try and increase flexibility in order to increase the options for learning open
to him. Such flexibility, it is suggested could only be effectively pursued by
acquiring an awareness of your own learning processes, in order first to establish which processes you do not currently employ, and then to establish how far
it might be possible for you actually to experiment with those processes. This
could be an attempt not merely to get closer to the ideal learning cycle, but to
get closer to full effectiveness as a manager by becoming a better learner.

The learner who is aware of his own learning processes, and aware of the
options open to him, is much more likely to be capable of directing his own
learning instead of being subjected to direction by others. He would then be
closer to the real sense of being a self-directed learner, and the next chapter
details the variety of methods by which the learner can achieve this desirable
goal.

Questions

1. Choose one or two recent learning experiences, and think about why you learned from them.
   - Why do you think you were motivated to learn?
   - Have you thought about what was involved?
   - Which of the Kolb categories are represented by these experiences?
2. Does one of the theories summarized here attract you more than the others? Why?
3. Do you think it is useful to you to think about theories of learning and motivation?
4. Can you identify specific actions you could undertake as a result of reading this chapter?

References

1. Burgoyne, J. and R. Stuart, 'Implicit learning theories as determinants of the effect of management development programmes', *Personnel Review*, **6** No. 2, Spring 1977.
2. Skinner, B. F., *Beyond Freedom and Dignity*, Penguin, 1973.
3. Luthans, F. and R. Kreitner, *Organizational Behaviour Modification*, Scott, Foresman, 1975.
4. Kolb, D. A. and R. Fry, 'Towards an applied theory of experiential learning' in *Theories of Group Process*, Cary L. Cooper (ed.), Wiley, 1975.
5. Handy, C. B., *Understanding Organizations*, Penguin, 1976.
6. Guest, D., 'Motivation after Maslow', *Personnel Management*, March 1976.
7. Festinger, L. and E. Aronson, 'Arousal and reduction of dissonance in social contexts in groups and group membership' in *Group Dynamics Research and Theory*, Cartwright & Zander (eds.) 1968.
8. Revans, R. W., *Developing Effective Managers*, Longman, 1971.

5. The self-directed learner

Terms such as 'self-organized learning', 'self-development', and 'self-directed learning' are increasingly found in current literature about management development. The terms are not strictly differentiated by their users, and it will be helpful if I give my reasons for choosing the term 'self-directed learner' first, and then use the information available from people who use the other headings, as appropriate.

The importance of self-direction

My emphasis so far in the book has been on the uniqueness of the individual manager. I have said that his environment, his personal make-up, and his past experience especially combine to produce the kind of behaviour which makes him the manager he is, yet require him also to be in some sense a better version of what he is. His learning needs, like his job, may be interpreted in some ways as being generalizable, but in other ways his learning needs are unique. I have also argued that, whether you think in terms of the inner causes of a wish to learn (motivation) or in terms of capacity actually to undertake a meaningful analysis of learning needs, the manager himself has the major contribution to make if either analysis or implementation are to be truly effective. While it is possible for some needs to be identified by the manager's boss or a management development adviser, and methods of meeting those needs can be devised and suggested to the manager, it is highly unlikely that real learning will follow unless or until the manager incorporates these suggestions into his own understanding and becomes committed to them.

Given the amount of training which is provided without seeking—let alone achieving—such understanding and commitment, it is probably necessary to restate and clarify this argument. I am not saying that others do not have a contribution to make to helping a manager recognize his needs. I am not saying that all training events run without active participation by the trainees in deciding their needs, and in devising solutions, will be useless and ineffective. I am saying that 'needs' and 'implementation' produced without effective individual participation will be flawed to some extent. (I will argue in chapter 9 that off-the-job training, particularly, still fails to recognize, or at least to meet, this need. Presumably it is too frightening to recognize the implications of, for example, spending as much time reviewing needs at the beginning of the course as we do preparing action plans at the end of it.) I am also arguing that many of the really significant needs which a manager has can only be effectively identified and met with his active involvement. This is particularly true in the area of interpersonal relationships. A manager may be hurt, but is not damaged, if he is told by his boss that he needs to know more about market research. If he is told that his relationships with other people are poor, he is likely to prevent damage to the self that really matters to him by finding ways of denying the need, or avoiding implementation, or sabotaging the learning process.

Since some readers may be struck by an apparent parallel with issues like participative styles of management, consultative versus autocratic managers, or democracy in industry, I should also make it clear that the case for self-directed learning is based on the principles of effective learning, and is not directly related to these apparent parallels.

It is also important to state what many managers know unconsciously. Most formal education is built on accepted truths—about science, history, sport, and so on. Truths are conveyed from teacher to taught. Teachers direct learning in both content and method. Managerial truth, in contrast, is fallible, contingent, unsystematized. Unlike students, managers can and must choose what to believe. They can therefore direct their own learning in the ways I now indicate.

A definition of self-direction

A manager is in control of his own learning in a crude, negative way. Like the horse taken to water, he can decide (even if he is hot and thirsty) that he does not want to drink. Managers are quite frequently placed in a formal training environment, where it is suggested that they should learn. Quite frequently, because they do not feel particularly hot or thirsty, or because they do not believe that what is offered will quench their thirst, they do not drink. In that sense, a manager controls his own learning. It is inconvenient to recognize it, difficult and uneconomical to act on the recognition, but all purveyors of training or education for managers recognize it in part. Usually, however, they recognize it as a problem for a minority on their courses—the unmotivated manager, the power-seeking autocrat—rather than accepting that all managers decide how much they will learn.

Negative control of this kind is only one part of self-direction. There is the positive sense, implied in the use of 'direction', the sense in which the manager can choose positively rather than reject. Chapter 3 suggested a number of ways in which a manager can identify his own learning needs. The success of others in attempting to direct his learning is likely to be limited, and this provides a pragmatic reason for attempts to increase the manager's own contribution. It is also the case that serious attempts by organizations to identify the learning needs of their managers are relatively rare, so that a manager who assumes that it is his organization's responsibility to look after his learning needs may well find they are not looked after at all. (See, for example, Walker and Gutteridge.[1]) There is, of course, another reason which will be attractive to some —namely the right of the individual to control his own self and therefore his own learning needs. The right may well be expressed in terms (self-actualization, autonomy) which are no longer as respectable as they were before further research began to chip away at Maslow. I think that the terms actually used, and the research base, are less important than a recognition that a person owns himself in a way which no employer can, and that he has a right to reserve to himself issues about himself. He is not a piece of machinery, he is a person.

Again, it is not convenient for many managers or employers to recognize or articulate that the manager has an ethical, as distinct from pragmatic, right to direct his own learning. Very often, neither has thought about the issue, which may well have been concealed by more politic expressions. A manager who says 'I do not think that is quite my kind of thing,' may well actually mean 'I do not choose to be interfered with in that way.' It suits both parties not to raise the issue of principle. Manager and boss may be unaware, or they may deliberately collude. Direct conflicts on this issue are extremely rare, in my experience. The point is worth making partly because some of the newer styles of self-development seem to side explicitly as strongly with managerial autonomy as older style courses do implicitly with employer autocracy.

More relevant still for readers of this book is the fact that a manager who involves himself in his own learning needs, in seeking opportunities to learn, in choosing particular learning processes, is more likely to find himself in conflict with some of the values and traditions of his organization. He is more likely to be aware of the difference betweeen comfortable (to him and others) learning needs, and uncomfortable learning needs. He is more likely to ask why his organization provides some learning opportunities and not others. He is more likely to ask embrarrassing questions of those who are supposed to help him learn. He is less likely to accept that what his organization says his learning needs are is a sufficient or acceptable statement. In short, he is more likely to recognize that directing his own learning may be pragmatically desirable for the organization but also inconvenient to it.

Fortunately for everyone's peace of mind, for many managers there will be an effective congruence between what the individual wants and what the organization wants. The point may, however, be particularly relevant not so much to the general mass of managers, but to the particular kind of manager likely to be reading this book, who is perhaps more likely to be interested in thinking about himself in depth and therefore more likely to recognize possible conflicts of interests.

To me, therefore, a definition of self-directed learning has to embrace both the pragmatic and ethical issues. It has also to accept some limitations on the capacity of the manager to direct his own learning—limitations of practicality rather than ethics. I do not regard the issue of whether a manager should be allowed to choose a form of learning which might damage him as a really live ethical issue. The pragmatic problem of presenting him with the information from which he can make a choice is much more relevant. The issue is not so much whether, for example, a T-group might damage a manager, but how he would get enough information to know whether it might damage or might help him. The problems of choosing a method of learning to suit capacities they cannot assess is illustrated by Harrison,[2] who shows both the excitement and the difficulties of the attempt.

Self-directed learning seems to me, therefore, to have the following dimensions:

- The idea that fully effective learning depends on the manager's participation in agreeing both learning needs and learning solutions
- The idea that there may be differences between the views of the organization and the views of the individual
- The idea that a manager who subcontracts responsibility for identifying and meeting his learning needs deserves what he gets
- The idea that giving the manager the right to choose is meaningless and irresponsible unless he is given data on which to base his choice
- The idea that learning involves being able to behave differently, in a way sought by the learner.

Self-organized, self-developed, or self-directed?

A general theme common to all these descriptions is that the manager should be responsible for his own learning. We do not need to go into detail on the origins of this general shift of emphasis away from organization-led or teacher-led philosophies of manager learning.

I believe that two different waves of thought became merged. The McGregor/Maslow psychology, essentially optimistic in its view of the willingness of people to take responsibility for themselves and to seek personal growth, became associated with a style of teaching, similarly optimistic at base, which emphasized that participation should be employed not merely as a style within a management education method, but as a choice between methods. Thus, not only should a subject be taught by involvement through discussion, but students should be able to choose whether to acquire the knowledge by that kind of discussion, or by lecture, film, or book.

The common issue, whatever the particular label, is how to help a manager to take the responsibility for his own learning. The most generally applied label is 'self-development'. Unfortunately, this is a description which has no commonly accepted meaning. Pedler et al.[3] define self-development as 'personal development, with the manager taking primary responsibility for his own learning and for choosing the means to achieve this'. They also comment that there are a large number of alternative definitions. This definition contains the essential 'responsibility for his own learning' point, but is unfortunately tautologous in its use of 'development', and therefore omits definition of what is meant by 'learning.' The definition also seems to me to over-emphasize the role of the manager in choosing the means for self-development; while I certainly favour increasing his contribution to the choice, it seems to me unlikely that, in practice, we can ever give him enough data for him to be given 'primary' responsibility in any real form. Most managers will, in practice, share the responsibility with their boss or a specialist adviser.

While, therefore, a lot of useful work is coming out of the self-development movement, and it is a term which I have used myself in the past, it now seems to me that the term is too imprecise for my purposes in this book; thus my preference for 'self-directed learner'.

One alternative is the concept of 'self-organized learning' advanced by Thomas.[4] He takes an important step forward by describing what is involved in being a self-organized learner. In his view the requirements are:

- The ability to develop criteria for success
- The power to evaluate one's own performance
- The ability to identify learning needs
- The ability to plan learning against those needs
- The capacity to review your own learning processes.

The useful feature about this list is that it takes us into the crucial area of what a learner actually *does*. The problem of accepting his term and definition is, however, precisely that the abilities he states as requirements seem to me significantly in excess of those likely to be possessed by most managers. His term may be a useful description, but it is a description of subset of learning managers, both because it proposes standards which are too high to be practicable for most managers, and because it really describes only one style of learning. Thomas's self-organized learner has more in common with the reflective observation style, and perhaps with the abstract conceptualizer (and therefore with the assimilator) than with the concrete experience/active experimentation mode (the accommodator). Since we know that managerial behaviour is more often active and experimental than analytical and reflective, we would suspect, even without Kolb's research, that the analytical/reflective style of learning would not be common among managers. Thomas himself proposes an industrial tutor who would draw up a 'learning contract' with the manager, support him through periodic reviews of his progress, and help him develop his learning skills. It would be an unusual manager who would offer himself in this way, an unusual employer who would pay for it, and an unusual adviser who could provide the right support. Thomas's approach seems to me, therefore, too near to a counsel of perfection to be useful guidance for most managers.

Learning styles or learning skills?

Categories of the kind developed by Kolb are a convenient shorthand. They are, inevitably, generalizations formed from clusters of particular approaches to learning. As Kolb says, each element is a necessary part of a total learning style, but people tend to give greater weight to one element rather than another. The categories are helpful, in my view, mainly to the extent that they cause someone to look at his own learning style and to understand it better; understanding it better, however, really ought to mean that he understands his likely response to a specific learning opportunity or event, rather than that he sees himself as an abstract conceptualizer or an accommodator. Otherwise his understanding is likely to be at an unhelpful level of generalization through which a manager has been able to apply a label to himself without being able to identify what he can or should do differently or better (a similar problem arises with other typologies, such as Theory X or the 9.1 manager).

As I have said earlier in this book, the apparent simplicity of statements of management style is understandably attractive to many managers, particularly if they find themselves in a category which carries current cachet. If, however, the manager stops at the level of acquiring a label, it is unlikely that he will have learned enough to be a more effective learner. Effectiveness is matter of particular behaviours; style is a general statement about a collection of behaviours. Some managers may make useful learning steps if they take a New Year resolution to become assimilators as well as accommodators. Most managers are more likely to benefit from deciding to add specific behaviours to their range (the result of which may, in fact, help them to be, for example, assimilators as well as accommodators). On the whole, I see 'styles' as a convenience for explanation and for association. Managers might question the utility of further analysis: I suggest that there are four reasons for a manager to look at his learning style and, as I will argue, his learning skills:

- Curiosity (which is, however, a short-lived and not very productive reason)
- A wish to understand how to extract maximum benefit from his learning style
- A wish to experiment with different learning styles
- A wish to make better use of learning opportunities which involve a learning style different from his normal style.

Skills involved in effective learning behaviour

It seems to me that, instead of the skills of learning described by Thomas, we need to look at a larger number of skills to be found across a range of learning styles. Some of these skills have already been stated in this book but not identified as skills of learning; others appear here for the first time:

- The ability to establish effectiveness criteria for yourself
- The ability to measure your effectiveness
- The ability to identify your own learning needs
- The ability to plan personal learning

- The ability to take advantage of learning opportunities
- The ability to review your own learning processes
- The ability to listen to others
- The capacity to accept help
- The ability to face unwelcome information
- The ability to take risks and tolerate anxieties
- The ability to analyse what other successful performers do
- The ability to know yourself
- The ability to share information with others
- The ability to review what has been learned.

I will not repeat the discussion of what is involved in the first three of these, since they have been detailed in chapter 3. The skills represent an even more formidable list than that given by Thomas, which I criticized as being beyond the likely level of most managers. I am not saying that a manager needs all these skills to justify seeing himself as an effective learner. I am suggesting rather that my self-directed learner is capable of working out which skills he has, and which he needs to work on.

The ability to plan learning

My own broad categorization of learners (which, of course, has the limitations mentioned earlier) is that managers are either *planners* or *opportunists*. Some plan careers, complete with sideways moves, promotions, experience in particular countries or functions, experience under a particular manager; they look for specific opportunities, although some kinds of opportunity (e.g., a prestigious course) may be more welcome than others (e.g., an in-company group learning project). They plan experiments with their own behaviour. Planners are, I believe, the people whom Thomas labelled 'self-organized learners'. Certainly, I see these planning behaviours as desirable for the self-directed learner, and a manager who has not been used to planning his learning in this way ought to think about whether he could add this kind of behaviour to his repertoire.

The ability to take advantage of opportunities

In contrast to the previous skill, some managers are opportunists; they rely, in practice, on accident or the planning of others to produce career moves, to suggest learning opportunities, to take the initiative in proposing learning events. In an important sense they do not match my description of the self-directed learner, since they are so much at the mercy of events and of other people, and rely too much on a benevolent organization to do the right thing for them. Given that they do not initiate, however, their skill in response is an important attribute. The ability to welcome and make use of learning opportunities as they occur is, of course, particularly crucial if you are not planning for yourself. The opportunist does not plan to get involved in a project, but once involved squeezes it for learning. He takes advantage of the situation to learn more about a subject, to observe and learn from the skills of others, to study the reactions of those with whom he and others interact.

The ability to review your own learning processes

Most managers have some basic ideas about the particular activities through which they have learned in the past. Their ideas tend to be about events rather than about processes—they talk about a job they did, a boss they had, a course they went on, rather than about what actually happened from a learning point of view. Kolb's ideas on learning styles may ring bells with some managers—and, of course, the idea of looking at learning processes through particular behaviours is exactly what we are doing in this section of the chapter. I have given my reasons for saying that this is a desirable thing to do, and therefore that it is a desirable skill for the self-directed learner. Not all managers may want to study their learning processes, however. Many will be initially more attracted to looking at the specific learning activities in the remaining chapters of this book, preferring concrete illustrations to relatively abstract learning processes. I hope this chapter will show that it is really possible to look at your own learning processes in a specific way, and that you do not have to be an abstract conceptualizer to be attracted to and benefit from it.

The ability to listen to others

I have already referred to some of the difficulties involved for a manager in accepting help from others. The skill I am talking about here covers more than the area of listening in order to be taught. There is a mass of evidence on how ineffective formal lectures are at conveying information. The special problems associated with lectures are, however, repeated in a slightly different form in normal day-to-day managerial communication. Many managers do not get as much from what is said as they need to for the effective conduct of business, let alone for the purposes of learning. They miss cues which would tell them about their own behaviour, about the reactions of others to them; they miss the things that have not been said and misunderstand things that have been said. The skill of listening is a crucial learning skill, and the lack of it explains why real time learning is often ineffective. I cannot give as much space here to listening as I would like, but it should be helpful to give four suggestions about what an effective listener does:

- He concentrates on what others are actually saying rather than making assumptions about what they should say, what they are bound to say (because of who they are), or what it would be nice to hear them say

- He recognizes and controls his own feelings about the person speaking, both as an individual and as what he represents
- He finds ways of checking his own understanding directly with the speaker
- He keeps his own speaking to the minimum rather than the maximum.

An effective listener learns because he knows more about what is going on. He also learns because listening is a form of flattery which causes others to offer more, from which more can be learned.

The ability to accept help

The capacity to ask for help in order to learn to be more effective seems to me to be associated with either the reflective observation or the concrete experience styles of learning. The request for help can be direct, with the manager asking someone to explain or demonstrate or give information. It can be less direct—for example, when a manager asks someone else to comment on something which he has done. If a manager asks someone 'What do you think about the way that meeting went?' he may be concerned to get feedback for managerial purposes ('I think the union will settle'), or for personal comfort ('You handled it very well'). The same question could, however, have learning objectives, representing a genuine underlying wish to find out if there was something he could have done differently and better.

Some managers do not ask for help in learning to be more effective because they do not know they have a need; they do not know they have a need because of earlier failures in analyses (see chapter 3) or feedback. On the whole, managers are not very skilled at asking for help, and they are even less skilled at offering it. It ought to be possible to ask for help from boss, colleagues, and subordinates directly and unambiguously, but many managers find it difficult because of perceptions of competence and status, and because of the widespread inability to face unwelcome feedback about individual performance.

For a variety of reasons, most subordinates do not ask their bosses for help, and are not provided with occasions when they could do so comfortably (see chapter 3 for my earlier comments on the problems of appraisal). The self-directed learner seeks opportunities.

We will be looking in more detail in chapters 8 and 10 at how a manager can seek and use help from others. The point to establish here is that the self-directed learner does not exist in a cocoon within which he determines his own learning needs and solutions. He is self-directed because he chooses what to do as a result of reviewing data from a variety of sources, and chooses what kind of help he needs to try and meet his learning needs.

Since other managers are, in my experience, very ineffective in giving useful feedback, it is essential to make the point here that the learner will need to help them give him useful information—he has to organize their help to him. He has to make it clear that he wants hard data rather than soft comments, and particularly that, at least to start with, he wants information on which he can base a choice on what to do rather than suggestions of what to do. This is, perhaps, a relatively unusual concept for many managers. The reason for this approach (collecting information before suggested solutions) is obvious enough when stated: that otherwise the solutions are based on someone else's perceptions, not on those of the manager himself.

One other issue about asking for help worth identifying here and developing in detail in chapter 8 is to review the reasons why critical feedback is often rejected, and why, therefore, opportunities both to identify the need to learn and actually to learn are missed. We commonly reject criticism from others:

- By trying to deny the validity of the data
- By questioning the competence of the critic
- By imputing (if only silently) impure motives to the critic
- By suggesting that the specific situation or behaviour is not typical
- By denying the objectives implied by the criticism
- By claiming that it is impossible in general, or impossible for us in particular, to change in the direction indicated.

The effective learner manages his behaviour so that he reviews rather than rejects criticism, as I suggest in the next paragraph.

The ability to face unwelcome information

In my work with groups of managers, I frequently find that they claim that their boss is only interested in good news, and reacts unhelpfully to bad news. My observations of behaviour supports this view. This has implications for both what we might call managerial learning and for personal learning. A manager who is not able to face unwelcome information does not get to know enough about his performance as a manager or as a person. To be told that you are not as effective in some ways as you think you are and know you need to be is not pleasant, and it is understandable that the information is often rejected. While not all unwelcome information is valid or helpful, the effective learner will tend to start more often from the position that it may be right than from the position that it is probably wrong. If someone says that he finds you patronizing or arrogant, it is more useful to think about what you are doing to cause him to say it than to excuse yourself by thinking about his personal deficiencies (e.g., insecurity and slowness of thought).

The most unwelcome information is that you have failed or been unsuccessful in some respect; the effective learner faces this information as something from which he can learn rather than something to deny. He asks questions of himself and others about what he has done, why things have gone wrong. Of course, not all unwelcome information is given in a spirit of caring for the person who receives it, a fact I have seen illustrated many times in business and most memorably on stage in Albee's play, *Who's Afraid of Virginia Woolf?*

The ability to take risks and tolerate anxieties

Gardner, in his elegantly written and exciting book, says:

> One of the reasons why mature people are able to learn less than young
> people is that they are willing to risk less. Learning is a risky business, and
> they do not like failure.[5]

We have seen in the previous chapter that people differ in their psychological
make-up in terms of their willingness to accept the risks involved in recognizing
and attempting to meet their own learning needs. Here we are concerned with
the kind of behaviour the effective learner will display. One illustration of
taking risks is contained in the theme of this chapter. It is more comfortable to
stick to the learning processes with which you are familiar and through which
you have been successful than to experiment with new approaches which,
because they call on new skills and new ways of behaving, contain a risk of
failure. The risk in listening effectively is that you will receive unwelcome
information. The risk in facing up to unwelcome information instead of dis-
counting it is that your self-concept is challenged. The risk in asking for help is
that it exposes your weaknesses.

The effective learner manages these risks, and his anxieties about them, by
recognizing them; he behaves as someone who knows about the risks and
anxieties and shares them with those who may help to reduce the problem. He
reduces risk by taking a risk. He reduces the risk of being seen to confess a
weakness, for example, by sharing with his boss the problem he feels he faces in
taking that risk.

The ability to analyse what other successful performers do

The self-directed learner has the capacity to observe and analyse what
behaviours other managers employ with successful results. Instead of learning
solely from the effects of his own activities, he is able to extract from the
behaviour of others examples of behaviour which he could employ himself.
This is not a matter of simple imitation, but of selective imitation. The actual
implementation is called 'modelling' and is a very strong feature of learning for
many managers. Not all managers, however, do learn this way, not because
they are unable or unwilling to imitate but because they do not have the ability
to study what others are doing—to undertake the style of learning which Kolb
calls 'reflective observation'. Managers who do have this ability show through
their behaviour that they are as interested in what others do as they are in what
they do themselves. They will reflect and ponder on what has happened in a
meeting and why, collect information (views and opinions) about what has
happened, discuss what has happened with others. Compared with others, they
may be listeners rather than talkers.

There is an associated, perhaps separate, skill which I would call the power
of disengagement, the skill of observing and participating at the same time.

J. W. Gardner says, 'By middle life most of us are accomplished fugitives from ourselves'.[5] Some elements of learning need are relatively easy for a manager to recognize; it is not particularly hurtful for most managers to recognize that they do not have a particular kind of experience or skill that they have never had the opportunity to acquire. The difficult parts of learning are those which require a manager to accept that he is not as good as he thinks he ought to be. Thus, some of the problems of cognitive dissonance, or avoidance of risk, of rejection of help which we have covered earlier arise.

The Delphic Oracle, on being asked for help, is supposed always to have given as the first answer 'Know ye yourself'. Learning is difficult when it touches the essence of a manager's concept of himself, and when it seems to raise issues of whether a manager behaves as he does because that is the best way to behave or because that is the only way he is. All learning for adults involves self-honesty, and some of the most important learning probably involves a frightening self-honesty. Most of the learning identified in this book does not require a huge disturbance of self-esteem (but some disturbance will be a lot to some managers). The manager does, however, have to make some judgement about how far he will go in attempting to know himself.

As we saw in chapter 4, one school of learning theory says that behaviour is all, and inner motivations are to be ignored because they are untestable. I have argued that both aspects need to be considered, but I feel that just as some managers can learn through relatively 'unthinking', unreflective processes, so some managers will learn more effectively if they know more about themselves, what makes them 'tick'. This point of view is expressed by Carl Rogers,[6] who said 'We cannot change, we cannot move away from what we are, until we thoroughly accept what we are'. He goes on to argue that we protect ourselves not only by not looking at ourselves, but by not trying to understand what other people say, because 'If I let myself really understand another person, I might be changed by that understanding'.

The behaviour of a manager who is really seeking to know himself is bound to be analytical and self-critical, instead of being evaluative and condemnatory of others. Knowing yourself as a precursor to learning involves, for example, assessing the ineffectiveness of your own communication rather than criticizing the motives or intellectual capacity of someone who has received the 'wrong' message. Knowing yourself means recognizing that you never, in your own mind, lose an argument. Knowing yourself means recognizing that the things you do are the things you like doing, not the things that make life better for someone else.

Knowing yourself is a constant process. It is important, powerful, and can be dramatic. I have seen managers acquire a level of self-recognition reminiscent of Saul on the road to Damascus. A lot of organizational development literature encourages this kind of process, for individuals and for groups. I believe I recognize the constructive and fulfilling nature of what is being attempted, but I do not accept that for most managers self-knowledge has to be acquired at the level of inner cleanliness suggested by Rogers. The learning manager needs some self-knowledge, but he should beware advocates who might take him so far as to disable him as an effective manager.

The ability to share information with others

Just as some people have ingrowing toenails, others have held their cards so close to their chests that they have ingrowing cards.

Managerial learning is essentially a social rather than a solitary experience. A manager who tries to assess his own learning needs without reference to the views others have of him is unlikely to identify them accurately. Learning is helped, therefore, if the manager is able to disclose relevant information about the actions of himself and others to others. The emphasis here is on the word 'relevant'. Managers disclose a lot of information to others for a variety of reasons, but they less frequently share information which would be helpful in securing more effective action; too often, information is doled out grudgingly, or important information is held back, or the information exchanged is essentially gossip ('Did you know X is going to get the job?'). The information disclosed by the effective learner is information about himself and his real opinions and feelings, not just facts and figures. It is the offering of information in difficult, sensitive fields—for example, about the manager's assessment of his own contribution—which brings out information from others which can help his learning process. Effective learners will often, therefore, take opportunities to share information about events with others, in an attempt to add to understanding about those events. For example, as Steele[7] says, they can exchange openly information on their views on the performance of colleagues instead of allowing each manager to work to individual standards in isolation (or, in my experience, receiving indirect and inaccurate feedback from others).

Of course, the true picture can be experienced as uncomfortable and unwelcome—which is why the learner needs the ability to face unwelcome facts. Sharing should also be undertaken normally by agreement and explanation of the process; to share information which the recipient is not used to receiving can be at least embarrassing and sometimes damaging.

The ability to review what has been learned

Although courses often include a session on what has been learned by the participants, and the latter are also often asked to write a report in which they may assess their own learning as well as the course, it is otherwise rare for managers to review what they have learned. Managerial life is usually seen as too oriented to immediate pressures and results for mangers to have much time to spare in looking backwards. I believe that, like many assumptions about management, this is a myth. There is a great deal of heart-searching and recrimination about failures, but it is too often designed to identify a culprit (preferably someone other than the senior manager involved) rather than to identify lessons. Successes are examined for learning even more rarely—partly because of an understandable impatience with the idea, and partly, I suspect, because examining the causes of success would sometimes show how fortuitous success was. It is more comfortable to sustain the fantasy of what has gone into a management success than to learn from the reality.

Reviewing what has been learned is obviously a reflective activity, of which many managers have little experience because of the environment in which they work and because of their preferred learning style. The manager who undertakes this kind of review may do so through some kind of group process or by undertaking a more solitary self-analysis. A number of versions of organization development encourage the former, while the Coverdale approach to decision making and team work can, in my experience, be an excellent vehicle for setting up a regular review of team processes and what the members have learned about working with each other, in a form of *post mortem*. The more solitary forms of reviewing learning are a matter of conscious self-discipline, undertaken either after particular events or at particular stages of an individual's career. The 'self-reviewer' looks at what he has done (for example, in a meeting), to see what he has learned from the experience. What information has he acquired—about the process, about himself, about the reactions of others? What has he learned about strategy and tactics? What has he learned about effective and ineffective forms of behaviour? The manager can secure help in highlighting or reinforcing, what he has learned by having a discussion with perhaps one other participant, instead of the full group mentioned above. This kind of *post mortem* has the great benefit of being part of a live learning cycle, rather than the dead end the phrase suggests.

The idea of a daily diary to help in analysing learning needs was discussed in chapter 3; a similar approach can be used to help a manager clarify and reflect on what he has learned. He can keep a diary of significant events during the day, noting against them either what he learned from the event, or what, in hindsight, he might have learned (see chapter 8).

Pursuing flexibility in learning behaviour

I believe that some aspects of learning behaviour are more easily added to an existing style than others. I think that behaviours close to those already used by the manager are more likely to be adopted by him. For the majority of managers, who like to dive in and learn by doing, I see little point in struggling to provide additional learning behaviours which emphasize theories or concepts, yet many academic learning processes do exactly that. For most managers, the kind of behaviour which would most expand their capacity to learn is centred on analysing the experiences of themselves and others. I should emphasize, however, that by this I mean reflecting on real behaviour in personally experienced work situations, rather than the (useful but less typical) occasions presented through case studies or role playing on a course.

I do not think it easy for managers to stand back and think consciously and regularly about their experiences, given the simplistic pressures on them to act managerially rather than to think about the results of acting. It is, however, relatively easy to start with a small experiment. If a manager feels that reflective learning has not been part of his normal armoury ar work, he could decide to give himself five minutes after the next meeting he attends to answer the following questions:

1. Who was the most effective contributor at the meeting?
2. What did he do that made him effective?
3. Which things did he do that I do not do as well as him?
4. Which things could I try out myself?

Developing the skills of learning

I have already said that nobody is likely to possess all the abilities outlined above. The self-directed learner:

- Is conscious of the learning skills he has, and those he does not have
- Controls his own decisions about improving or adding to these skills
- Increases his feeling of confidence in taking the risks involved in learning by deliberately seeking to develop his learning skills.

Perhaps the most important requirement for a manager who wishes to develop his learning skills is that he should be able to escape from the shackles of his own experiences of learning. So often managers are unnecessarily limited in their approach to learning because they are trapped by conventions made by themselves or their environment. The learning manager has the effrontery to challenge the conventional wisdom, even when it is his own.

In the First World War, British (and French and German) generals could only think of one way of winning the war, which was to slog through trench warfare. Lloyd George had the ability to think sideways, to try and find other ways of winning. The approach to thinking christened by De Bono 'lateral thinking' has the same characteristics, and is one way for a manager to escape from his own traditions on learning.

While describing the importance of escaping from unnecessary conventional shackles, it is also important to emphasize that, for many people, learning styles are more likely to be subject to modification, not reconstruction, to evolutionary step-by-step transition rather than revolutionary change. Also, we have again to remember the influence of environment on learning; perhaps Lloyd

George was able to think unconventionally because he was outside the generals' environment.

Handy[8] has made an interesting attempt to associate particular kinds of role culture with the kind of approaches to learning encouraged in those cultures or organizational styles. While his book is more useful in describing a situation than in helping a manager whose learning style does not happen to fit that favoured by the organization in which he works, it does stress the point that a learning manager does not exist in isolation from his environment. Any change in his learning style has therefore to be chosen with an understanding of, and perhaps as a result of negotiation with, the environment in which he wants to experiment.

Age and learning

We have some inappropriate views about the relationship of age to learning. Young managers are supposed to learn, but older managers are thought to be past it, either in the sense of need or capacity. It may well be that older managers respond better to particular methods of learning, especially to those which will enable them to deploy and test their experience, rather than to those which require them to listen to formal statements of principle by others. I think there may well be a problem of expectations rather than actual capacity, that older managers do not expect to learn and it is not expected of them. More widespread changes in managerial employment in recent years have shown that if the motivation is there (e.g., the need to acquire new skills following redundancy) the ability to learn survives much longer than was previously thought. If, however, the manager is largely inexperienced in learning, or unused to the particular methods used, learning will prove difficult.

Perhaps the most important aspect of the relationship between age and learning is that, as with many other skills, learning is sustained by constant use. (See, for example, modern research on the maintenance of sexual capacity in later life.) If a manager allows himself to get out of the habit of learning, he will find it difficult to pick up new learning. Age is not an absolute but a relative factor; if you are out of practice, learning will be as difficult at forty as at sixty. The self-directed learner may well find that his job after a period of time ceases to provide relevant learning opportunities and new challenges. Thus he may arrive in a situation in which his organization no longer requires him to learn, but he wishes to learn in order to keep his learning muscles in trim. He may therefore need to press at the boundaries of apparent opportunities within his organization (assuming he does not choose to leave it) or, as some managers do, seek opportunities outside the organization which may not be seen basically as learning activities but in fact fulfil that function. Examples of this include voluntary work, where a manager's organizational abilities may be welcome but where he has to adapt to the different objectives, methods, and personalities involved.

Questions

1. Which experiences in your working life have been most relevant to your success as manager? Can you relate these to a learning style?
2. How far has your learning been directed by your own conscious decisions, and how far by accident or the decisions of others? Is that the way you want it to be in future?
3. Which skills of learning do you believe you have (see the list on page 86)? Which skills do you think you might be able to add, or to improve?
4. How far will the environment (boss, traditions of the firm) help you to change your approach to learning?

References

1. Walker, J. W. and T. G. Gutteridge, *Career Planning Practices*, American Management Association, 1979.
2. Harrison, R., 'Developing autonomy, initiative, and risk taking', *European Training*, **2**, No. 2, 1973.
3. Pedler, M., J. Burgoyne and T. Boydell, *A Manager's Guide to Self Development*, McGraw-Hill, 1978.
4. Thomas, L., 'Learning to learn in practice', *Personnel Management*, June 1976.
5. Gardner, J. W., *Self Renewal*, Harper and Row, 1964.
6. Rogers, C., *On Becoming a Person*, Constable, 1961.
7. Steele, F., *The Open Organization*, Addison Wesley, 1975.
8. Handy, C., *Gods of Management*, Souvenir Press, 1978.

6. Opportunities for learning

So far, I have tried to establish the context for the manager who wants to learn—the content of his job, the ways in which he can assess his own effectiveness, the psychological processes involved in learning. In this chapter I want to look at the opportunities available for learning, and to do so in the light of the following convictions:

- In many organizations, opportunities to learn are restricted less by the capacity of the manager to learn from a particular event than by the preconceptions, prejudice, and ignorance of those responsible for managing learning opportunities
- Many opportunities for learning are not recognized, or if recognized are badly used
- Planned learning is more effective than accidental learning
- Most opportunities occur through real work situations, not through formal training events
- Managers vary considerably in their ability to see the value of potential learning opportunities.

The choice of phrase 'opportunities for learning' rather than the conventional 'methods of learning' is a deliberate one. My reason is partly that 'methods of learning' carries with it overtones of a process outside normal managerial activities, whereas 'opportunites for learning' gives more of the flavour which is at the centre of this book, of taking opportunities which exist in the manager's real world. In addition, I see the identification of opportunities as the primary task, the choice of method the secondary one (just as it is in other aspects of business life).

Are opportunities given?

In a 1978 survey,[1] Guerrier and Philpot found that less than half their sample of more than 1300 British managers thought that managers in their organization were given an opportunity to develop their full potential and skills. Further, only 28 per cent of managers in larger organizations (10 000 people or more) gave this response. Both figures are significant indicators of the failure to provide opportunities; the lower figure in large organizations may be due to a number of factors, possibly including a greater recognition of the learning opportunities which could be provided.

A study of the published work of British bodies such as the British Institute of Management, the Central Training Council, the Industrial Training Boards, the Manpower Services Commission shows a constant message; management development is essential and not enough is being done. For a variety of reasons, the learning needs of managers are either not being diagnosed, or if diagnosed are not being met.

What opportunities?

The opportunities for learning are now well recognized. My own list, which emphasizes opportunities rather than methods, is:

- Real time learning: learning where the task is the main focus, learning is subsidiary
  —Unplanned learning through current job
  —Planned, created learning within current job responsibilities
  —Planned, created learning by adding to current job responsibilities
  —Planned, created learning by special assignments
  —Planned, created learning by experience outside work
  —Planned learning from the boss or colleagues
- Off-the-job learning: learning where the experience is designed for learning
  —Courses, seminars, workshops
- Off-the-job learning: other methods
  —Reading
  —Other non-work experiences.

Examples of learning opportunities

We will be looking in detail at each type of learning opportunity in later chapters, but in order to illustrate the points made in this chapter I give some examples here which should make the different kinds of opportunity clear.

Unplanned learning through current job

This is the kind of experience through which people learn but only recognize they have done so after the event. Most management learning is of this kind. One example is that of a manager who was given responsibility for dealing with union representatives for the first time, and found that the militant senior steward effectively controlled the meeting by calling for an adjournment every time the other union representatives seemed to be shifting from the line he wished them to take. He learned by trial and error how to avoid allowing an adjournment until he had established at least a partial agreement.

Planned learning within current responsibilities

A manager found that one of his subordinates, although highly competent in presenting a report or a case on paper, lacked confidence in his ability to present the same information orally. He therefore asked his subordinate, while continuing to do his normal written reports, to give him an oral summary each week of the main features of the reports, and gave him helpful comments and suggestions. He then arranged for his subordinate to do the same thing to a monthly meeting of his colleagues.

Planned learning by adding to current job responsibilities

A manager of a company whithin a UK-based multinational was identified as the potential successor to the director of the product division in which he worked. The division had seven units in different countries, and was about to set up a small unit in France. The manager had no experience of working outside the UK, and it was decided that the setting-up of the French company would give him a learning opportunity relevant to his future career; he was therefore appointed as joint general manager, with a Frenchman, while retaining his existing UK job.

Planned learning by special assignments

A manager who had previously been involved wholly as a finance manager was given an additional responsibility for purchasing, which had previously been run by a long-service manager who had worked by personal contact, past history, and files in his head. In the past 18 months, there had been a very significant cost increase for the bought-in containers in which the product was packed. One of the first priorities for the new manager was to find alternative sources of supply, or an alternative form of container. It was thought that if the manager undertook a tour of other companies in his group who used containers in some form, he could both acquire useful information about alternative containers and also acquire information about how they set up and managed their purchasing function.

Planned learning by experience outside work

A number of organizations in both the USA and the UK are taking advantage of opportunities offered by voluntary organizations who need either part-time or full-time executive help in running their work. Managers can be seconded from their normal business to set up or administer particular projects, which can give them opportunities for learning in various fields outside their previous experience, and also experience of having a level of responsibility which they may not previously have had.

Planned learning from the boss or colleagues

I am not talking here about the currently fashionable topic of the boss as coach, since I treat this later as a method rather than as an opportunity for learning. I am thinking of the role of boss or colleagues as models, people whose style and methods can be observed and learned from, either positively or negatively. Chairmanship at meetings is a managerial skill often acquired by modelling. The study of the behaviour of effective colleagues is also a major source of learning.

Off-the-job learning by design

Courses, seminars, and conferences specifically designed to provide learning are familiar enough not to need illustration here.

Off-the-job—learning by other methods

Most people have some experience of learning from reading, although there are great limitations to what can be learned for managerial purposes from reading unless it is associated with some other learning process involving action. Many managers do not realize that, as I show in a later chapter, reading outside the immediate technical or managerial area can be very fruitful in producing analogies for managerial problems—for example, in using fiction to understand more about the roles people actually play.

The opportunities offered by various forms of voluntary work on committees are more usually seen by managers as social opportunities or duties than as the learning opportunities they could be.

Choice of opportunities

Most of the approaches which claim some novelty are in fact derivations of one of these opportunities, although the fervour with which some 'new' approaches are proselytized tends to conceal that fact. One of the problems about helping managers to learn is that, for reasons of effectiveness in the learning process, we have tended to separate the learning activity from other managerial activities, in order both to highlight and to improve the learning process. In so doing, we have too often failed to identify and make use of the opportunities which occur as an inherent part of normal managerial life. Some of us have also been seduced by apparent analogies with professional occupations into giving too much importance to learning occasions structured on academic, teacher-taught lines.

If managers could be given the learning experiences they need in neat teaching packages in a controlled environment, the task of learning would be much more simple. However, even if such packages were available and effective in learning terms (i.e., managers actually learned what they needed to), it is unlikely that the vast majority of managers would be willing or able to take advantage of the packages. The Rose Report[2] estimated that only eight per cent of managers in the UK experienced a significant off-the-job training event in any year. Even if one takes the most pessimistic view of the appropriateness of the educational product actually available as compared with the potential market for a really attractive product, it is clear that for most managers in most organizations, learning off the job is an unavailable or very occasional learning opportunity. In those firms where regular attendance at courses is a cultural norm, the percentage of a manager's time so spent is unlikely to exceed five per cent in any one year.

Some people argue, in any event, that management education and training off the job through courses is fundamentally inappropriate and useless, and that managers will only learn through real work experiences. While there are good reasons for saying that much management training is at best unproven and at worst proven to be ineffective (see chapter 9 on this), it is unfortunate that those who wish to sell their own brand of management learning should find it necessary to knock other brands. Although the reading of knocking copy can be highly enjoyable, except for those whose product is being criticized, I fear that the process is disadvantageous to the overall cause of management learning, since it tends to reinforce general scepticism rather than really to encourage the sale of a particular product. The search for ultimate truth in management learning is, in any event, premature at this stage of our investigation of various methods. We do not know enough about the comparative results secured by different methods to presume to state with arrogant certainty that coaching, action learning, self-development, or a high quality business school programme are the one true way. The pride of ownership of those who have invented or discovered these approaches is understandable, but we should not confuse pride and Messianic fervour with comparative evidence.

Managers and those who advise them on learning opportunities should be looking to assess the whole range of learning opportunites and seek to employ as many as possible rather than to identify one method as being the sole solution. By this I do not mean that learning opportunities should be sought and deployed indiscriminately, but that the values of each should be assessed in relation to particular needs; it will probably be found that in many cases a combination of approaches could sensibly be used to tackle a particular need. As an example, let us look at the case of one manager, Brown, who had been appointed as general manager of a medium-sized company within a larger group of manufacturing companies. Brown had been appointed to this position from a series of jobs in sales and marketing. Among his problems in his new job was the fact that he was, for the first time in his managerial career, responsible for production, a function in which he had no direct experience, and on which he had received no training. He and his boss decided that he could not be a fully effective general manager without improving his knowledge of production and they went to some trouble in attempting to define what kind of knowledge about production he needed. In summary, the areas they identified were knowledge of the process by which plastic sheets were transformed into the product, knowledge of the way in which production was planned and controlled, and knowledge of how maintenance and production should interact in the most cost-effective way.

(The reader might like to pause at this point, take a blank sheet of paper, turn back to the brief summary on pages 99–101 of the different varieties of learning opportunity, and note which kinds of learning opportunity are available to this general manager.)

In practice, learning opportunities are rarely assessed in the way used through the box exercise above, for reasons which are discussed later in this chapter. In most cases the manager would learn, if at all, through unplanned, accidental experiences in the normal course of his job. If the need were properly identified then, despite the seniority of the person concerned, it would probably be answered in some firms by looking for a course on production techniques, or added to the general list of areas of knowledge required which leads to someone being sent on a general management course where he will be given sessions on manufacturing policy. In other firms, the manager would simply be advised to spend more time on the shop floor looking at what goes on, and chatting to the most experienced production foreman. The problem with these answers is not that they are wrong but that they use insufficiently the range of opportunities potentially available.

The reality of reality

I have already given one reason for giving preference and weight in discussing learning opportunities to real time learning; the fact is that most managers will, in practice, have few other opportunities. There are, however, substantial positive virtues in using real time experiences as the basis for learning. For managers, such experiences have the special advantage of being the real thing, not a lecture, role, or case divorced from reality. They also have the advantage of offering the opportunity to learn by doing, rather than by listening or by the kind of analytical process which is foreign to the normal life of most managers, so that in this sense, too, they represent the manager's real life, rather than being an artificial or conceptual abstraction of it. They also offer the opportunity to base learning on a meaningful task so that the manager can feel comfortable with the task (a familiar managerial event), rather than uncomfortable with a learning process which is not his normal mode of behaviour. Finally, the opportunities can be geared to the actual tasks and problems of the individual manager; as I have shown in chapters 2 and 3, these individual requirements are crucial to the provision of relevant learning.

This, then, is the good news about using real time learning opportunities; the bad news is that it is not easy to make effective use of such opportunities, partly because the manager is constantly tempted to give most of his attention to the task in which he is involved rather than to the process of learning from it. The other reason for the difficulty in using these opportunities is that it is often difficult actually to structure the learning experience in advance in a way that both assists the learning process and facilitates monitoring after the event to see how effective the learning has been. We will be looking in detail in later chapters at ways in which these problems can be overcome.

The oddity of learning through real time opportunities is that learning from experience is the most frequently quoted source of learning, yet any analysis of the learning opportunities available in managerial jobs shows that the opportunities are rarely taken up consciously and are often ignored altogether. We will be looking at some of the reasons for this later in this chapter.

Make do with make-believe

Courses are at the opposite end of the scale to real time learning. Although many modern courses do attempt to provide learning experiences based on the performance of a task—crossing a river, building a tower from paper, measuring the size of a car park—the situations are essentially artificial, attempts to simulate real managerial life rather than being real managerial life. Courses have the great potential advantage of having been designed as learning vehicles, so that the problems of confusion of priority and purpose which arise in real time learning should be less present. In some cases, there is no confusion at all, because the kind of learning experience offered (such as a lecture or case discussion) contains nothing but a learning experience (if indeed it contains that). In other instances, as the learning experience moves closer to reality (as in the task-centred examples given above), confusion between task and learning objectives again arises, as the learners get caught up in the joy of the task and descend reluctantly (and often rather badly) at the tutor's insistence to the review of what they have learned.

Unfortunately, course organizers have attached their course processes too often to concepts of involvement, participation, activity, and learning by discovery because of a partial understanding of the fact that managers like to be active, and that they like doing things which at least resemble things they do in their normal work. In the process, tutors may often have given a reasonable representation of the chaos and confusion which is the reality of much managerial life without actually providing a good learning experience.

The special feature of courses as learning opportunities—that they can be designed to meet a particular learning requirement—can therefore easily be thrown away in a confusion of activities and purposes related to a half-understood desire to simulate reality. Moreover, courses often fail to pursue the kind of reality which would be most useful to many managers. One of the clichés often used by managers about a course experience is that it gave them the chance to stand back and look at themselves and their jobs, an opportunity which we know is not easily available to them on the job (chapter 2). Course organizers do not do enough to capitalize on this aspect of reality to, cause managers to spend time on material brought by them from their real world, instead of studying material brought by the tutor from another world. The relevance and effectiveness of many courses would be improved if managers brought with them relevant material—objectives, job descriptions, time analyses—and used the opportunity given by the course to apply new thinking and new standards to this material. Many courses have ventured into the area of helping managers acquire self-knowledge of their effectiveness in social interaction; few give them the kind of learning opportunity which would involve them in a real study of themselves as managers of resources, of themselves, of their own time.

The failure to recognize opportunities

At least two managers are involved in recognizing opportunities: the manager himself and his boss. In many organizations, a staff adviser—personnel, training, or management development—may also be involved in at least some of the formal processes for identifying learning needs and solutions, through appraisal or some formal approach to analysing the learning needs of groups of managers. Yet when we look at the learning opportunities actually provided, we find that in many organizations they are frequently either accidental, through changes of job or boss caused by organizational pressures which have nothing to do with learning, or they are dominated by one particular approach to satisfying learning needs.

Of course, some organizations look as if they are using all the possible methods, and a talk with their central management development adviser may well convince you that they have heard of everything and tried most. In fact, it usually is the case that particular divisions have experimented with particular approaches and are just as limited in what they do as autonomous companies of comparable size tend to be.

The reasons why opportunities to learn are not recognized can be summarized as below:

- There is a tendency to repeat the known and successful instead of looking for new ways of learning
- The people concerned lack previous experience of an activity as a learning opportunity
- Managerial work emphasizes single-purpose activities, rather than multi-purpose activities, including learning

- Managerial work tends to be hyperactive, and to concentrate on doing rather than thinking
- The psychological make-up of some managers discourages the identification of opportunities.

Known and successful

The British civil service has, at least since reforms in the nineteenth century, been dominated in its approach to learning for senior staff by the provision of experience through job rotation. Through this method, the bright administrator enters from university and is put through a series of experiences in which he progresses through grades with defined responsibilities, and through a number of sections within the major department in which he works. In the Department of Employment, for example, he would work at different times in separate branches concerned with safety, health, training, employment services. The aim would be to give him a wide variety of jobs as he worked his way to the top, so that when he got there he would know something about everything which his department handled. Only with the Fulton Report did the civil service add a significant leavening of training off-the-job to this approach for senior administrators. Frequent moves also meant that the opportunities for developing an effective relationship for learning purposes between manager and subordinate (not terms used in the civil service) were inhibited in some respects.

It is also increasingly recognized that many organizations which pride themselves on the attention they pay to management development seem in practice to give exclusive attention to devising management training courses or to making carefully weighted choices of which business school or similar institution to patronize (in both senses of the word). Thus, organizations will become famous for being dedicated to the managerial grid, or to cadre training, or to interactive skills training, or to a range of sensitive experiences generally labelled organization development. Both organizations and individuals tend to repeat what they believe to be successful, to be playing one instrument when they could be discovering the pleasures of an orchestra.

Lack of previous experience

Perhaps even more significant than the general limitations of an addiction to a particular method is the general absence of effective use of opportunities to learn through normal job activities, which I have outlined earlier. If asked to describe how they have learned their managerial job, most managers will describe the jobs they have done, and what they have learned during each job. It is a paradox—and, for those of us who want to help managers, a frustrating paradox—that, although with hindsight they recognize the fact of learning on

the job, they find it very difficult to identify these opportunities in advance of their occurrence, either for themselves or for others.
Thus:

'In that job I had my first experience of dealing with government departments.'

'I was given a special assignment, looking at the cash flow consequences of the spring inventory build-up. Then they turned me round the other way and told me to look at ways of preventing the build-up.'

My boss had alway said the meetings were such a waste of time that there was no point in both of us being there. When he was ill and I had to go, I learned a lot of things which improved the reports I did for him.'

In each of these cases, the managerial decision about who should be involved and how was made entirely on task performance grounds—how a particular task could be undertaken most conveniently or effectively. Yet each case provided an opportunity for learning as an easy, inexpensive, not time-consuming adjunct. In fact, in each case some learning was achieved, as an accidental byproduct; but if the learning opportunities had been defined and discussed in advance, so that the manager involved could attempt to plan and monitor his own learning processes, it is likely that he would have learned more. It may also have been the case that in the first two illustrations the decision to give someone a task may have been incorrect from the point of view of giving the learning opportunity involved to the person who needed it most or could benefit most from it. Unfortunately, it is difficult to help managers to escape from this paradox of recognizing learning *post facto* but being unable to plan for it. Since the main source of learning is from experiencing something, and they have not experienced the planning of learning opportunities, they have not learned how to learn. Ways of tackling this problem are discussed in chapters 7 and 8.

Learning by planning and by hindsight

Partly because managers miss so many opportunities to plan learning experiences, many learning opportunities actually occur in retrospect. A manager who has had a stimulating or harrowing experience may recognize after the event that he had learned something, although he may not have planned to do so. The opportunity may sometimes be seen not as an opportunity to learn, but an occasion for rationalization, in which the real nature of the experience is softened or explained away. The learning experience occurs when there is a genuine attempt, perhaps aided by the manager's boss or a consultant, to reflect on the experience and identify what happened as a means of deciding future action rather than as a means of avoiding unpleasant conclusions about what happened.

107

The role of the boss or some other helper in assisting the manager to identify these retrospective learning opportunities is crucial, not only for the immediate experience but because it can lead to similar opportunties being identified in advance on a future occasion.

Single-purpose activities

Managers tend to concentrate on one activity at a time, on one objective rather than others, on one purpose for a single activity. Thus they prefer to be told, for example, that either their cost objective is paramount, or that quality is, that getting an answer is more important than whether you upset the person of whom you have asked the question. Given this pattern of belief and behaviour, it is not surprising that the idea of tasks containing learning opportunities, with objectives which can be spelled out and results which can be monitored, is one which is not only foreign to their experience but antithetical to their normal style of behaviour. Even the explanation that learning can be very much a secondary objective is likely to be received with some impatience, and a clear indication that the adviser who is identifying learning opportunities is living in a world far removed from the reality of the manager's job. Again, more than one paradox is present, not only because, as mentioned earlier, learning does occur in some cases, but because in fact managers' behaviour does frequently have more than one objective or purpose, despite their frequently articulated wish that they should only have clear, simple, unitary goals. In practice, managers have both task and personal objectives. For example, they want to convey certain information, and they want to do so in a way that gives greatest credibility to themselves; the task of conveying the information is therefore planned and managed in a way which it is hoped will succeed in meeting both objectives. Managers constantly demonstrate their desire to kill two birds with one stone, but only when they see both birds as rewards; learning is not often seen that way; as we have seen in chapter 2, achieving tasks is rewarded in a variety of ways, learning rarely is.

Hyperactivity

As I demonstrated in chapters 2 and 3, managers tend to be hyperactive, to be doers rather than thinkers, performers rather than reflective analysts. The identification and planning of learning opportunities could in theory occur well in advance, as in the case of changing somebody's job, or be done closer to the immediate opportunity—e.g., 'John has called a meeting on the Hovis account in ten minutes; what do you think my line should be?' In either case, an element of analysis would be required to identify and then make use of the learning opportunity, and busy managers are not in the habit of doing that kind of analysis. The general climate in favour of getting things done, rather than planning to get things done, militates against doing more than the immediately obvious tasks and against those things which are seen as marginal to the important demonstrations of managerial role. Learning and the provision of learning opportunities for others are not seen as giving such a demonstration.

Psychology of some managers

In addition to the general reasons likely to influence the ability of managers to identify learning opportunities—some of which, of course relate strongly to the organizational environment in which they work—there are reasons to be found within the individual make-up of the manager himself. We looked in chapter 5 at some of the characteristics of the manager who learns, as compared with the manager who does not. Obviously, some of the characteristics can be identified further back in the learning process, at the stages when needs are identified and opportunities are sought. I have not been able to find any research evidence showing which managers seek out learning opportunities and which do not, so the views I express here are anecdotal, drawn from the experience of myself and others.

Some of the categories are crude and may be thought obvious. Elderly senior managers who have existed with some success in stable environments are not likely to identify learning opportunities for themselves; they may talk about never being too old or too senior to learn, but such talk never seems to lead to any identifiable action, unless it is to expensive conferences in warm climates from which they return with actions that other people should undertake. Such managers are usually not good at identifying opportunities for their subordinates, either because of their own inertia or through fear of improved competence among those below them.

At the other end of the scale, bright young managers can be equally impregnable to the prospect of identifying learning opportunities; high fliers can become remarkably complacent about the possibility of further learning once they have been through the special christening rites appropriate to bright young managers in their organization—the two-week country house course, the assignment as PA to the chairman. MBAs represent a special case, since they spend so much time struggling to get into jobs in which they can apply what they learned at Harvard, London, or Cranfield that they are often disinclined to look for additional learning experiences.

I find the greatest problem is with those senior managers who are young enough not to be completely solidified in their ignorance, yet who have reached a level of seniority in which learning needs would be genuinely difficult to identify and who are influenced by the generally held belief that managers at their level ought not to have any learning needs. For such people, the identification of needs can seem like a criticism of their current performance, or a hint that they have flaws which will prevent further promotion. The

109

psychological barriers inhibiting these managers from looking for learning opportunities are accentuated by the fact that there are likely to be very few models available to them of people at senior level who have had their career or life enhanced by learning once they had become senior managers.

Perhaps the largest number of managers with psychological barriers to identifying learning opportunities are in Hawdon Hague's phrase 'the needlessly impotent', who quote the boss, the structure, the organizational climate as the reason for their refusal to take the risks involved in recognizing that opportunities to learn could usefully be sought. Significant as these factors are as partial explanations, as we saw in chapter 1, it is still the case that for some managers they are excuses and rationalizations. The managers who have said to me 'there is no point in learning to be more effective because . . .' certainly needed help, both personally and organizationally, to take advantage of learning opportunities without the fear that they would be derided or punished for doing so. Most of all, they needed help to recognize that they did not need to give up.

To recognize learning opportunities, managers—young, old, middle, junior, or senior—need to have the following characteristics:

- They must be capable of being dissatisfied with their current level of performance, or with their knowledge, skills, or attitudes
- They must be capable of recognizing that managerial activities can have more than one purpose
- They must believe that it is possible to learn by planned direction rather than by accident
- They must believe that the culture in which they work, and particularly their boss, will give them some support, and some reward
- They must believe that recognizing learning opportunities will lead to an improvement which they desire to make.

The responsibility for identifying learning opportunities

The manager himself has the main responsibility for identifying learning opportunities; who else has the level of interest which he should feel in improving himself? If it is also accepted that many opportunities will occur within the existing job, the manager is himself very well placed to identify them.

This does not mean that, in practice, managers carry this responsibility very well. They often tend to feel that their boss should be looking for opportunities for them, or that someone in personnel or management development should be doing so.

It is, indeed, desirable that the manager is helped by others, partly because they may actually be aware of opportunities which the manager himself cannot know about. They may have been informed about organizational changes, business problems which needed to be studied, requests for help from other departments in the organization, requests for nominations to external committees. They may also be able to help by spotting opportunities which are within the manager's view but which he has not seen, particularly in helping him to see those situations in which the main activity contains the potential for learning as well as task achievement. Most personnel and management development people are better at helping with the first kind of opportunity, because they belong to the right kind of information net and because it is part of the system and bureaucracy by which they collect the points which they need to justify their existence in most organizations; they are less effective at the second, because they rarely know enough about the detail of the manager's job and are not usually able or willing to get to know enough about it. Whereas personnel people can broadly be expected to be interested in helping a manager to learn, the same is not necessarily true of the boss; there can be an incongruity between the individual's interest in identifying opportunities and the interests of his boss that he should stay as he is, conveniently performing well enough not to threaten the boss.

The manager's boss can be very effective in identifying opportunities within his area of knowledge, which will usually be deeper but less wide than the personnel man. Where he particularly can contribute is in knowing about opportunities in and around the manager's existing job, because of the knowledge of relevant activities which he possesses. He can also help because his knowledge of the strengths and weaknesses of his subordinates sometimes causes an activity to register in their mind as a learning opportunity for Mr X because of the specific association, although they might not have thought of the activity otherwise as a learning opportunity. One of the most frequently encountered examples of this is the decision to involve a subordinate in something in which he has not previously been involved, as the following example illustrates.

> The normal arrangement in a firm of heating and ventilating engineers was that the senior manager in the contracts department always dealt with tenders for contracts of over £1 million in value, and personally negotiated any changes in the basis of tender. One of the consequences of this was that his subordinates, who dealt with smaller contracts, had no experience of dealing with those of the clients who concentrated on large contracts. When these companies moved down-market at a time of recession, the more junior managers in the contracts department were faced with a need to deal effectively with more sophisticated and sharper contacts. The senior manager decided to take each in turn with him when he did his large-scale negotiation.

The responsibility for providing learning opportunities

Normal managerial life is teeming with opportunities to learn, which the manager himself can take without the need for any help or intervention in terms of seizing the opportunity (although he could well benefit from help in trying to get the most out of the opportunity). The first responsibility is therefore the manager's own, to make sure he is taking advantage of what exists.

For the reasons given in this chapter, bosses are not as good at identifying opportunities as it would be desirable for them to be. When the opportunities have been identified and provided, they then face the familiar problems of priority; most learning experiences, even when basically on-the-job, involve some extra commitment of time, at least for the manager himself to review what he has done and what he has learned. In many cases, the boss ought also to be involved in this review, helping to ensure that the manager has learned from the opportunity provided. (See the section on coaching in chapter 8.) Those opportunities which require a significant absence from normal work—assignments, special learning projects—are unpopular. The manager who is motivated to learn must therefore help his boss to do the right thing by giving him good reasons for agreeing—by working out how any change in his work pattern for learning purposes can be accommodated without discomfort to the boss. Ideas on how to deal with this difficult problem are given in the next chapter.

Another significant responsibility of the boss is to provide learning opportunities by giving to, or sharing with his subordinate, parts of the job carried out by the boss. This kind of learning opportunity has not been dealt with in this chapter since it is only a version, although an important one, of the ways of learning on the job. Detailed examples of how this can be managed are given in chapter 7. The other form of learning opportunity provided by the boss, again dealt with in detail later, is the effect of the boss as a model which I mentioned at the beginning of the chapter. In most cases, the opportunity is not so much provided in the planned sense, but exists in the sense that what the boss does can be studied and used as either a positive or negative exemplar.

Conclusion

This chapter, while summarizing the wide range of learning opportunities potentially available, has emphasized the reasons why the opportunities are not properly utilized. Just as too much management education and training has been built on inaccurate statements about what managers do, so too many statements about management development have consisted of lofty statements about the responsibilities of managers for identifying learning needs for themselves and their subordinates. Until we recognize the kind of real world in which managers live, our prescriptions for learning opportunities will remain unattached to what the manager believes he can do. Now that we have looked at both the opportunities and why they are not recognized and taken up, we can move on to a rather more positive level in the remaining chapters, and look at how these opportunities can be used.

Questions

1. Which learning opportunities do you think have had the most impact on your development?
2. How many of the types of learning opportunity listed on page 99 could be available to you in your current job?
3. Which learning opportunities are most relevant to meet the personal needs you identified at the end of chapter 3?

References

1. Guerrier, Y. and N. Philpot, *The British Manager: Careers and Mobility*, British Institute of Management Foundation, 1978.
2. Rose, H., E. Newbigging and D. Clarke, *Management Education in the 1970s: Growth and Issues*, NEDO/HMSO, 1970.

7. Opportunities to learn through job experiences

Learning from experience?

This chapter and the next deal with those learning opportunities which managers would tend to call 'learning from experience'.

Managers, when they talk about learning from experience, nearly always mean learning from doing a job, and usually also mean to draw a distinction between that and learning from a formal training course. As we have seen earlier, all learning is in some sense learning from an experience, but it is not always very fruitful to use this kind of wordplay with managers. However, I want to avoid perpetuating a misunderstanding about the word 'experience', and I certainly do not want to encourage any tendency to see learning from experience on the job as 'real' learning, and learning from activities off the job as another kind of learning; which of the two would be seen as dubious or second-rate forms of learning might depend on whether you are an academic or a manager. Hence my preference for the description used as the title of this chapter.

When managers talk about learning from experience, they mean that doing a different job, or being given new tasks within a job, or working for a new boss, or interacting with new colleagues, all provide different situations. If the situations are handled successfully, learning is assumed to have occurred. In fact, at the time, the manager may not recognize that he has learned something because—as we saw in the previous two chapters—few managers go through a careful, reflective, analytical process to establish what they have learned. Usually when managers talk about learning from experience, they are looking back from some event where they have applied a piece of knowledge or skill which they only recognize they have learned after they have applied it successfully. For most managers, planned learning from a job experience is a relatively rare phenomenon, because the idea of planning this kind of experience is both untraditional and foreign to some aspects of normal managerial learning behaviour. I will go on to argue that there is no need for this kind of planning to be so rare. First, however, I will suggest ways in which unplanned learning can occur, can be encouraged, and can be used most effectively.

Turning opportunities into results

All the examples given in this chapter concentrate on describing the opportunity rather than the total process involved. The next chapter will look at the ways in which opportunities can most effectively be turned into learning results. At this stage it may be helpful to give some indications of the necessary steps:

1. The manager himself must recognize that an opportunity exists to learn, either before or after the event.
2. He must have the capacity to recognize that learning does not have to be a discrete activity, separated from normal tasks.
3. He must review the resources available to him to help provide the opportunity or to help him learn from it.
4. He should understand the extra benefits likely to accrue if he specifies learning objectives and attempts to measure results, rather than simply having an experience from which something useful may be learned.

Unplanned learning throught the current job

Unplanned learning opportunities I define as opportunities which occur without the learner being aware in advance that the opportunity may arise. The joke about the adult who studied English language as a subject and found that he had been speaking prose all his life is no doubt familiar. Much the same discovery can occur when managers are asked to review how they have learned; many of them discover that they have been learning ever since they started their career, without recognizing at the time that that was what they were doing. Yet the learning they have achieved is only a partial response to the rich opportunities which are present. I described in the last chapter why so many opportunities are missed. Basically the causes are lack of awareness of need, lack of motivation to learn, absence of support and encouragement from the environment, or, in some cases, failure to identify opportunities as opportunities because they are not recognized by the manager's predominant learning style. The potential learner who has gone through the analytical processes covered earlier in this book is, however, more likely to be equipped to take advantage of the unplanned opportunities which come his way. Some of them will still not fit his needs, motivations, or interests, but others will. Since the vast majority of learning opportunities will, in fact, occur unplanned, the learning manager (whatever his basic style) needs to be able to take advantage of them.

Even the manager best equipped to learn in this way may fail to spot the opportunities, so it is to this aspect that I will give attention first. The opportunity may be missed at the time, or in retrospect. It may be missed at the time the opportunity occurs, in the sense that the manager fails to spot the chance to experiment with his own behaviour, to observe someone else's behaviour analytically, to listen hard in order to acquire new information. It may be missed in retrospect, in the sense that a manager who has been involved in an experience not only did not recognize at the time that there were things he could do to assist his own learning, but also failed afterwards to review that experience to see if there was something to be learned from it.

Awareness of opportunity

Clearly, the first step most managers might take to increase the amount of learning is to enter activities with the consciousness that they may provide learning opportunities; the manager may not be able to specify in advance what the opportunities actually are, but a constant awareness that opportunities of some kind may come up would be a great facilitator of spotting specific opportunities when they do occur. Some managers, even though convinced intellectually that the opportunities will be there, find the process of spotting them at the time difficult. Their level of engagement in what is going on is such that they do not find it easy to participate fully in their normal managerial role and at the same time to distance themselves sufficiently to be able to observe what others are doing or to observe the reactions of others to what they are doing. This is, in fact, a particular case of the general problem I discussed in the previous chapter—that many managers see task achievement and learning as not merely different but separate processes. I believe this means that most managers will miss some opportunities, but not that most necessarily have to miss as many as they do. Awareness of the existence of opportunities is something managers can consciously develop; to do so would add significantly to their learning capacity. A manager is, after all, usually heavily engaged and interested in some things but not others, is highly skilled in some areas but not others, finds some issues difficult and others easy, already knows some facts and not others. Some opportunities to learn certainly can be seized around those areas where the manager is relatively relaxed by his existing level of knowledge skill or commitment. In short, the manager I described as the opportunist as distinct from the planner can optimize his opportunism by being aware that most activities in which he is involved give some opportunities to learn.

The nature of unplanned learning on the job

One of the reasons why opportunities are not spotted is that, although managers actually experience learning as something derived from their normal jobs, they tend not to think of their tasks as potential learning experiences. There is also a tendency when discussing opportunities in the abstract for managers to think of learning as strongly related to teaching; they tend to think about learning as something structured, a specially created experience, and also as something in which there is a 'teacher' and a 'student'. Unplanned opportunities for learning on the job are, clearly, different from these kinds of expectations. The experience available is unlikely to be structured even in part as a learning experience, nor is it likely that someone will take a teacher role. Unplanned opportunities are likely to depend either on personal experiment by the learning manager or on his analysis of the activities of others. They are not likely to be very efficient learning opportunities, in the sense of information or experience being carefully selected to meet the specific needs of the individual manager. They may be somewhat lonely opportunities, in that the manager may not have the support, help, or encouragement of others while he is trying to learn. They may be risky, hit-or-miss opportunities if the opportunity is for the manager to experiment (which is open behaviour) rather than to observe and analyse (which others may not notice and which therefore carries few risks).

Spotting unplanned opportunities

To advise managers that their normal work situation is teeming with opportunities to learn if only they look for them is only a first stage. Because so little of the learning process in real life opportunities is conscious, they have little experience on which to base their increased wish to spot opportunities. They also have the problem that an activity they have always thought of in one way is difficult to perceive in another way. It is not necessarily easy for them to see that an activity can be undertaken to achieve a main purpose (task achievement) but also meet a secondary purpose (learning). A manager appointed to a new committee may quite well understand that as a result his status is confirmed, his product interests are protected, his need for information is met. He may even generalize afterwards about the valuable experience he got from being a member of the committee. He is less likely to be able to specify things added to his knowledge or skill through his membership.

The following examples illustrate unplanned opportunities. (Many of them could with advantage to the learner equally well be turned into planned opportunities to learn, but for the moment we will deal with the kind of opportunities available to most learners most of the time.)

Experimenting with own skills

Many of us have rather inflexible behavioural repertoires; the way we behave in particular situations or with particular people becomes a matter of habit. The learning manager—either through a desire to experiment for the sake of experiment or because he has established a need to improve his performance—learns through trying different forms of behaviour. He either adds additional behaviours to his repertoire, or he finds that a new form of behaviour is more effective and allows another form to fall into disuse. The opportunity may arise because of a changed circumstance affecting his job.

Negotiating skill

A manager finds himself faced with a new negotiator unexpectedly at a contract negotiation with a supplier. On previous occasions, he has been accused of not trying to understand the supplier's point of view. He decides that, instead of listening to the supplier's case in order to establish which points he can destroy, he will listen first as objectively as he can, and then summarize his understanding of the supplier's case to the supplier before moving on to his own points.

Discussion-leading skill

A manager finds that his meeting has been shifted from its normal room with a long oblong table to another room with a square table. He cannot sit in isolation at one end as he normally does. Instead of regretting the absence of his normal environment he decides to find out after the meeting from his own feelings and by asking the views of others whether the new seating arrangement helped to influence the style of the meeting.

Analytical skill

A divisional marketing manager was given a copy of a report about a product in another division. He received the report from a colleague simply as a matter of interest. He decided to read the report and assess it in two ways. First, he would analyse it as himself to see which questions it answered satisfactorily, and which unsatisfactorily. Second, he would analyse it as if he were his functional boss, the company marketing manager, and see what difference there might be in expectations and needs at that level.

Receiving coaching

Managers sometimes receive direct help from bosses or colleagues in the acquisition of information, suggestions about a particular approach which might be adopted, or explanations about some information or process. Quite often, these are unsought, possibly unwelcome, and unplanned. Illustrations are:

A newly appointed manager was travelling with a manager who had previously worked in his department. The new manager mentioned that he was having particular difficulty in handling one of his subordinates; he asked his colleague for information about previous attempts to improve the performance of the subordinate.

A manager was finding it extremely difficult to decide whether some of the information being presented to him in the monthly management accounts was being doctored in order to provide a more favourable picture than the facts justified. He felt uneasy about directly challenging either the line manager or the accountant concerned. A more experienced colleague who received similar information from a subordinate level happened to be with him on the day the latest figures arrived. The manager put the problem to his colleague.

Analysing the behaviour of others

I talked in the previous chapter about the potentially powerful influence of modelling, of imitating the effective behaviour of others. I will be looking later at some of the more sophisticated analytical techniques for doing this, the use of which has, however, to be planned in advance. The kind of opportunities which occur unplanned include the following:

A manager felt during a meeting that the chairman was particularly good at controlling a running dispute between two long-standing rivals. Every time an explosion seemed near, something happened to prevent it. He decided to make notes of what it was that the chairman did, said, or caused to happen which had the effect of switching attention from the issue about to erupt.

A unit manager attended a meeting with his divisional boss in which the company's managing director received the division's budget and plans for the coming year. As they waited for the meeting to start, one of his colleagues complained: 'We are only stooges in this event. George will do all the talking and answer all the MD's questions, and we won't get a look in.' The manager was struck by the accuracy of this remark and decided that, instead of sitting in frustration, he would try to see whether there was a pattern to the MD's questions, and whether he would have answered them differently.

Identifying and planning natural learning opportunities

By 'planning opportunities' I mean thinking ahead about opportunities and deciding how to take advantage of them. The planning can be either entirely in the head or committed to paper. As I mentioned in the previous section, most unplanned learning opportunities can, in fact, be identified in advance if the manager has developed a habit of mind which causes him to think about the possibility of an opportunity being present. So one variety of planned learning opportunity arises from activities which will occur as a natural and inevitable part of the process in which a manager is engaged. As we have seen, meetings provide opportunities to behave differently or to analyse the behaviour of others; the presence of a colleague gives opportunities to get information or suggestions. These situations can be envisaged, and opportunities turned from accidental to planned situations.

The benefits of trying to turn unplanned into planned opportunities wherever this is possible may not be entirely obvious. It could be argued that if lots of opportunities are going to occur, a resolution to take advantage of them is all that is necessary. Busy managers may not favour having another burden suggested to them, and the benefits will have to be seen and experienced by managers in their own situation if they are to be convinced. The reasons why benefits may be present, and therefore why it is sensible at least to experiment with more planning of natural opportunities, are these:

- Thinking about what you are going to do before you do it quite often improves your performance.

To take the example I quoted of the divisional budget meeting, the manager knew before his colleague talked to him that he was likely to be unemployed. He could therefore have planned in the general sense 'What opportunities for me to learn might there be?' and then in the specific sense. He would have benefited from asking himself what sort of things to look out for, what kind of analysis to do, how to note questions from the MD, and the response he would have made to those questions.

- Setting objectives is just as useful and valid for this kind of activity as for anything else.

Looking analytically at how someone else is performing may be quite a good way of filling in time, and may give some learning. There may, however, be a number of things you could do to learn, and the easiest may not be the most important. The manager needs to know what learning he wants to achieve and therefore which opportunity to choose.

- Planning often involves co-operation.

It may be possible to get a colleague to help, and thereby add to or improve learning. Instead of deciding on the spur of the moment to try out a new style of behaviour and to monitor his own performance, a manager who plans to act in this way could ask a colleague what he thinks about the idea, or could ask a colleague to watch his performance and comment to him afterwards.

The reader might now like to test the two propositions I have suggested in this section, that many unplanned learning opportunities could be converted into planned opportunities, and that planning is worth while. Each of the examples given on pages 117–119 can be assessed to see how far it would have been possible for the manager to plan for the opportunity which arose, and what kind of benefits could have emerged from doing so.

Types of additional learning experiences

So far we have dealt with examples of planning to learn from opportunities which will arise as a natural consequence, but as a byproduct, of activities in which the manager is inevitably involved. We should now look at examples of opportunities which arise not from day to day, perhaps relatively routine, activities, but from involvement in other activities specially selected because of their potential in providing learning opportunities.

As I said at the beginning of the chapter, managers asked to talk about the events or processes from which they have learned will often highlight new situations or experiences—sometimes a new job, sometimes a new task added to their existing job. Some bosses are very good at providing, and some managers very good at seeking, such opportunities. I was fortunate enough to have fairly early in my career a boss who was very good at giving me new tasks and assignments from which I learned, and I was able to compare him with other bosses who did not provide similar opportunities in similar situations. The range of opportunities which can be identified and provided is extensive.

At one end are tasks which need to be done anyway but which may be given to X rather than Y in order to provide a learning opportunity to X. Examples are a manager asking a subordinate to draft a report, or to attend a meeting, or to visit a supplier. Such opportunities may be very much within the context of the existing job, but are added to it.

At the other end are activities which are essentially created as learning opportunities, although they have a major real task element and potential utility to contribute to a non-learning purpose of the enterprise in which they are undertaken. Examples are processes like Revans' action learning, or the Manchester Business School joint development activities, where useful projects are undertaken but the originating force is to provide a learning experience. In these cases, the manager is taken outside his normal job and perhaps is transferred to a new environment.

Between the two ends of the range, there are activities which are quite clearly added to the manager's normal job, but which occur with a strong task focus; special assignments or appointments to a 'task force' or 'project group' or 'review committee' are examples. This is learning from additional responsibilities.

One of the differences between the learning opportunities I am describing in this section and those I described at the beginning of the chapter is that the earlier examples were of opportunities which essentially were within the control of the manager himself to identify and utilize. The examples in this section clearly have a much stronger element of someone other than the learning manager identifying and suggesting the opportunity to him. It is in these examples that the boss and the management development adviser come into the picture. They are probably not sufficiently in contact to identify the kind of examples with which I started the chapter, and in any event they tend to be more concerned with larger-scale issues which carry greater apparent impact. As I have described him, the self-directed learner will not depend solely on those external agents, but will seek to identify and press for the kind of learning opportunities I am now going to illustrate.

Learning from additional tasks

I have always been in favour of the view of manager development as a horticultural analogy, in the sense of nurtured growth in a favourable environment. Views of development as sudden, explosive growth, or views of learning as a process in which a manager is manufactured by a mechanical process of carefully defined teaching inputs, attract me less. The idea of a manager learning through a gradual accretion of tasks around his central job core seems to me entirely in tune with what actually happens. It is not always a conscious process in the mind of either the learner or of his boss. In all organizations in which I have worked there have been tasks which did not fall inevitably onto the plate of any manager. Such tasks get distributed, often by work loading, equity, or just by first in the door gets the task. Less frequently, these tasks are explicitly awarded to the man who will learn most from undertaking them. Here are some examples of the kind of opportunity which is available.

A manager was required to send one of his subordinates to a technical conference to represent his unit. He did not select the manager who knew most about the subject, but selected the one he thought would benefit most from attending, although the subject matter was marginal for him. In addition, he asked the manager concerned to brief himself with the expert before going, and then to speak to a departmental meeting on his return.

A three-monthly report to the managing director was normally written by the divisional manager. At the beginning of one year, he told three of his unit managers that each of them in turn would write the report, so that each of them would gain experience of what was significant from a divisional rather than a unit perspective.

A finance manager reporting to a finance director normally did a commentary on the budgets submitted each year by divisions; the commentary was used by the finance director in budget meetings with the divisional directors. The finance director secured the agreement of the managing director that the finance manager should attend the meetings and participate.

A managing director who had previously been finance director retained his previous contacts with stockbrokers and financial analysts. His finance director was not familiar with all these contacts; a programme was drawn up for him to meet them.

Learning from additional responsibilities

Industry is still inclined to think of status, technical knowledge, political balance before it thinks of who could learn from additional responsibilities. Thus appointments to committees, working parties, review bodies, task forces are not sufficiently related to what a manager could get out of the experience. As I have already said, however, managers quite often fail to take full advantage of the learning opportunities involved even if they are appointed, because they are unaware of the existence of a learning opportunity coincident with the task or responsibility they have been appointed to perform. Even when appointed to act as deputy for an absent manager, it is rare for a manager to think of this in specific learning terms rather than vague pleasure or general awareness of the usefulness of the experience.

This kind of learning is therefore often unplanned, both in the sense of the general opportunity being sought by the learner or his boss, and in the specific sense that if given the responsibility the manager does not plan to learn from it. In the same way that an opportunist will take advantage of an unplanned learning opportunity within his current job, so he can take advantage of these additional responsibilities.

Here are some examples of these learning opportunities.

A committee was set up by a large multinational group to review the operation of its personnel policies, and to make recommendations for improvements. The political balance of the committee was carefully weighted, and it was decided to include one of four divisional directors. The obvious choice was a man who was based at group HQ, and had been a successful personnel director in another company. In fact, another director was chosen, who was expected to benefit more in learning terms from exposure to this level of policy formulation, and from exposure to managers of a different nationality than his own.

A managing director was concerned that, although much attention had been paid to labour productivity, insufficient attention had been given to utilization of materials. In selecting a task force of three managers, he chose one with little direct experience who he thought would benefit from involvement outside his functional area.

A company involved in pharmaceuticals had decided to investigate options for diversification outside that industry. The major content of the study was expected to be concerned with marketing and finance, and experts in these fields were appointed to the study group. In addition, a production manager was appointed, because it was felt that in his existing job, although in many ways an excellent performer, he was too narrowly concerned with production, and was insufficiently aware of how his function could most effectively relate with others.

The distribution function in one company had for many years been the responsibility of the production director. Shortly before he was due to retire, an organizational review concluded that it would be appropriate to leave the distribution responsibility under the new production director. The managing director, however, decided to give the marketing director the responsibility, because he wanted to give him the chance of learning what was involved in managing a function in which he was not technically expert.

A marketing manager was given the task of reviewing the reasons why inventory had for the last three years gone to a peak in the same two months, and proposing ways of eliminating the peak without causing some other significant problem.

A manager was asked by his boss to deputize for him while he was away on a four-week management course; he asked his subordinate to review with him beforehand the major problems he was likely to meet, and what he might learn during this period.

Learning from task experiences away from base

In chapter 1 I gave some examples of opportunities for managers to learn outside work. Some opportunities arise in social situations, some in apparently more business-like environments, such as committees. These are opportunities identified and used by the learning manager himself, and his employer may know nothing about them.

The employer is likely to be concerned when the opportunity involves an actual change of job. The opportunity which arises may not, in fact, be or be seen as a learning opportunity—it may be simply a means of parking a manager for a period of time until a new assignment comes up, or it may be seen as a way of giving a hard-worked manager a rest, or it may be a way in which those companies who have developed a social conscience meet the apparent demands of that conscience.

Opportunities of this kind are not always sought or accepted eagerly by career-conscious managers, who may be worried about the impact on their careers of significant periods of absence from the corridors of power. Secondment for two years to act as projects director for a charity may be seen as morally satisfying but potentially dangerous to a career. Attempts to encourage interchange between the civil service and industry in the UK have met with problems because industry is not well geared to both make and implement a promise about the career of a departing manager. Secondments or exchanges can be valuable, but are probably most easily managed by organizations with similarly efficient bureaucracies.

As a learning experience, taking up a job on secondment to another organization tends to have most impact on a general willingness to see that there is more than one way of doing things. It rarely adds managerial skill or knowledge likely to be of help to the manager directly within his sponsoring organization. (Civil service secondments into industry are more directly relevant to them than vice versa, especially if the civil servant moves into a section where knowledge of industry is crucial rather than merely interesting.) Secondment has, however, the potential to add to a manager's knowledge of how to handle new situations, new colleagues, different cultures, but too often these opportunities are not fully recognized and the learner receives little help in learning.

There is a further problem with secondments. They provide the challenge of a different milieu, an opportunity to be different, of working with and learning from a new boss and colleagues. Yet the learning required to be effective in the new environment will take much energy and attention; since these elements are often job specific, the secondment may not be a useful or efficient learning experience because the learning is not capable of transfer back to the sponsoring organization yet it occupies, because it satisfies immediate prime needs, the learning 'space' which might otherwise be available for learning more relevant to the sponsoring organization.

For the vast majority of managers, opportunities of this kind are not available; for the minority who may be given the opportunity, the message is to take advantage of it as a chance to learn, and not simply to treat it as another job in a different environment. This means seeking explicitly to get time and help to review and improve what the manager is actually learning, as well as setting specific learning objectives. Of course, it will be true that things are done differently in the new organization, but a manager who is only able to report on the what and the how rather than the why has missed a significant learning opportunity. Of course civil servants have a different approach to problems—the real learning opportunity is to see how they handle their conventions and their environment, and what skills they deploy while doing so.

Learning through learning projects

The approach to learning through projects devised by Reg Revans has claims to be the most influential approach to management learning in the UK in the last decade. The essential principle of his action learning approach is that managers learn by doing real work rather than by being taught in a classroom. It is I think important to recognize that Revans developed action learning because of his dissatisfaction with traditional forms of management education as he had experienced and practised them. Like Picasso, who was a powerful conventional artist before he developed his own style, Revans is an accomplished performer in the most traditional educational skills of lecturing and writing. His belief in the power of his own theories, and his distaste for other forms of management education is conveyed with splendid logic and fervour, and it is easy to be spellbound, as by a Messiah come to rescue us from the error of our ways. The story of the conversion of Sir Arnold Weinstock, normally thought to be unimpressed by management education, is a tribute both to Revans and to his method.

Revans's view of learning[1] has much in common with that of Kolb (see chapters 4 and 5). He sees it as essentially a scientific process of speculation, testing, and summary of learning. In his view, managerial learning is not an acquisition of new knowledge so much as a rearrangement of the old, and the rearrangement is best achieved by performing meaningful and risky managerial tasks and sharing the learning experience involved in the task with other learning managers (rather than with management teachers). Revans believes that the role of teachers is to contrive conditions in which managers may learn with and from each other.[2]

The essential feature of action learning, says Revans, is that managers should be dealing with a real problem; while most interest and excitement in the literature has been generated by managers being seconded to other organizations, Revans argues that projects dealing with familiar problems in a familiar setting should be the most frequent. Clearly, also in Revans's view, although not in the practice of some who have copied him, action learning emphasizes organizing managers during the project to learn from each other. Although action learning at GEC has included formal teaching of some subjects,[3] Revans himself seems to see little value in formal teaching, giving it a somewhat grudging mention.

Action learning as originally practised involved a major expenditure of time and money; the early GEC programmes stretched over eight months, with intensive work full-time on the project and learning about it. Not surprisingly, later versions elsewhere take less elapsed time, can be part-time, and involve much less devotion to sharing experiences in a group of learners.

There are now a number of versions of attempts to give managers learning projects, not all of them derived from Revans. The Manchester Business School approach, called joint development activities, has many similarities. Much less has been written about it, which is a pity because it seems to offer a bridge between different forms of learning provided through one institution.

It may be a source of either discomfort or pride to Revans that almost any management development effort involving a project, some academic input and a formal project report is called action learning. The struggle to balance a useful task with useful learning about learning seems, however, increasingly to be lost, with emphasis in these projects swinging back to the task. I am certainly not impressed with some of the efforts to do action learning on the cheap. The excitement of the project, and of sponsoring a learning activity which offers benefits to the organization other than learning, seem to me to have caused the learning benefits to be downgraded, so that those involved really experience a sort of untrained consultancy project.

There are fundamental problems with the learning project approach:

- If done properly, it is expensive. How much availability of learning opportunity should be directed this way?
- Although it involves real work, it is an analogy of part of the manager's job, not of the whole
- It brings into play skills many of which more resemble those of a consultant than of the normal line manager
- It is an answer to some of the problems of some managers, not the uniquely appropriate solution which some of its proponents suggest
- Project work has too often become a learning solution looking for a problem, a solution through which managers are processed without attention to their individual learning needs.

Making learning normal

I conclude from my analysis of the important and helpful efforts to set up learning projects that the invention of new experiences for learning purposes is not the most useful process in which those wishing to help managers learning should engage. The prime need is to help managers learn from their normal work experiences. We need to find improved ways of assisting managers to recognize how much they could learn from their current activities, how to kill two birds with one stone. Sir Thomas Beecham gave a marvellous illustration of the principle, when he described Herbert von Karajan as a 'sort of musical Malcolm Sargent'. Just as a double-barrelled joke can be doubly funny, so a managerial activity from which both task and learning results are drawn is doubly useful.

As I said at the beginning of this chapter, I have deliberately concentrated on further definitions and illustrations of opportunities to learn, and have said very little about how opportunities can be converted into actual learning. My reasons for doing so are likely to be convincing to those who agreed with, or are now prepared to accept, my general proposition that the crucial step for most managers is to see how many opportunities to learn exist without the need to manufacture special experiences. I hope my emphasis on opportunities without the distraction of methods of learning brings this out clearly.

The ways in which managers can take advantage of those real time learning opportunities are the next important focus for discussion, but a manager has to recognize an opportunity before thinking about how to take advantage of it.

Questions

1. Look back at your work last week; from which specific activities do you think you learned something useful?
2. Look again at last week's activities; were there things you might have learned if you had planned in advance?
3. Which of next week's activities offer you opportunities for learning?
4. Are you aware of projects, assignments, committee places which may come up shortly which might give you new knowledge and experience. Can you put in a bid for them?

References

1. Revans, R. W., *Developing Effective Managers*, Longman, 1971.
2. Revans, R. W., *ABC of Action Learning*, R. W. Revans, 1978.
3. Casey, D. and D. Pearce, *More Than Management Development*, Gower Press, 1977.

8. How to learn while managing

The duality of managing and learning

The previous chapter showed how numerous the opportunities to learn from job experience are; we need now to move to the issue of how best to take advantage of those opportunities. In many cases I will be describing the process by taking one of the opportunities illustrated in the previous chapter, and showing how that opportunity might be used. I will be concerned to show the processes available to a manager to learn while he is carrying out a task not wholly devoted to learning—how to learn from the many opportunities which may come his way without a learning label attached to them. I hope to maintain a realistic balance, so that I am not suggesting techniques which would optimize learning at the expense of effective task achievement.

It was claimed of one British Prime Minister that he said in a speech that it was silly to put the cart before the horse, or indeed the horse before the cart; since what was necessary was for horse and cart to be placed together. In most managerial situations, task achievement will be the major concern and learning a secondary adjunct. The important thing for managers is to recognize that it is possible to achieve both task and learning. The suggestions made in this chapter do not assume that it is practicable for most managers to make a major shift in the way they spend their time, but that there are ways of getting learning out of situations not requiring a total reorganization of work priorities.

The rational approach to learning

The most rational, best organized approach to learning involves processes exactly analogous to those a manager would hope to use on any other management process. He would:

- Collect data
- Set objectives
- Define standards of performance
- Plan activities
- Monitor achievement
- Review the reasons for deviation from standard
- Decide what additional action is necessary.

Of course, a lot of managerial life does not follow the neat sequence and controlled analytical thought processes required by the textbooks; since there are extra difficulties involved for managers in the relatively unfamiliar world of conscious learning, the likelihood of managers actually applying these disciplined steps to learning would seem slim. However, since some of the readers of this book are likely to be in the special category of managers who would like to follow this kind of approach, we will start with the ideal before adjusting to more common reality.

Collect data

If the manager has been through one or more of the processes described in chapter 3, he will have acquired data about his learning needs. His knowledge of his own preferred learning style may have been enhanced by chapters 5 and 6, and his awareness of learning opportunities sharpened by reading chapter 7. He then would have the data necessary in order to set some learning objectives for himself.

Set objectives

The last chapter mentioned the case of the manager who decided to find out what others felt about the results of a new seating arrangement at a meeting. If he had received data which suggested that he was seen as a remote chairman who brought members into discussion insufficiently, his learning objectives might have been:

- To learn whether changes in seating affected perceptions of him as chairman
- To learn whether those perceptions were the same as his
- To analyse the reasons for any difference in perception.

Define standards of performance

In the case of the manager who decided to change his strategy in negotiation, he would benefit from setting standards of performance which would measure his objectives of listening without interrupting, and summarizing the supplier's case. Such standards might be:

- While aiming not to interrupt at all, actually to do so no more than once
- To summarize the supplier's case so accurately that the supplier would have no major corrections to make to the summary.

Plan activities

A manager was moved into a new division in which most of his colleagues were new to him. He planned to visit each of them, and prepared a list of questions about the relationship between his unit and theirs, what problems had occurred in the past, and what might be done differently in the future.

Monitor achievement

The manager who decided to see whether there was a pattern to the managing director's questions at the divisional review in fact found afterwards that he had not done so very effectively. He had been impressed by the MD's approach but he still did not know why. He had taken lots of notes, but found it difficult to interpret them.

Review the reasons for deviation from standard

In the case just quoted, the manager decided that he had not achieved much for two reasons. He had not really thought hard about what he wanted to achieve, and his two objectives (studying the MD's questions and devising his own answers) were not really compatible, because he was thinking about answers he would have given instead of analysing the questions.

Decide what additional action is necessary

It may be useful to illustrate this question with two different kinds of learning review.

In the case of the divisional director who was appointed to the personnel review committee, the personnel director took an opportunity to ask him whether he thought he was learning anything from his involvement with the committee. It became clear that the divisional director had no idea of the real reason for appointing him, and thought that his appointment had been made purely to ensure that his divisional interests were protected. The personnel director gave him the reasons for his appointment to the committee (and took a note about how to handle such situations in future). This review shows the problems arising from a failure to communicate, let alone get commitment to, a learning objective; it therefore illustrates how specific action relevant to the particular case can also bring out general action points.

The second case is more of a piece with the earlier examples, in that it is the learner who reviews against his own plan to learn. It is the case of the unit manager who was given an opportunity to write the full divisional report. He decided that one experience was not enough, and therefore decided to review the divisional reports produced in turn by his colleagues, and to decide how he would have rewritten them in order to produce a more effective document. The additional action he had decided was therefore essentially to see learning as an extended rather than a one-off process.

A fully systematic and disciplined approach to learning would take in each of these steps, in this sequence, for each learning opportunity. Many managers will not, however, find this totally systematic approach congenial as an immediate approach. The reflective, looking-back elements involved will not suit many managers—who, nonetheless, can take advantage of at least some stages of the processes. The most significant step for many managers will be that of looking back at recent activities to see what opportunities for learning may have existed, and through that process to recognize that it would have been possible both to look for opportunities to learn in advance, and to plan how to take advantage of them.

Learning as a shared process

I have described, particularly in chapter 5, some of the reasons why managers find it difficult to identify to themselves, let alone to others, those areas of skill or knowledge in which they need to improve. To go further—to involve boss, adviser, colleagues, or subordinates in helping the manager to learn—may be seen as even more difficult. Yet for the manager who wants to learn from managerial activities in real time, it is very desirable to make use of the opportunities offered by the other major figures in his normal work environment.

Most of the ways in which other people can be used are well known; the problem is to devise ways in which more advantage can be taken more frequently. The ways in which others can help are basically:

- Helping to organize learning opportunities
- Providing an encouraging learning environment
- Monitoring what the manager is actually doing and learning
- Providing feedback on what the manager did or did not do, and on reactions to his actions
- Providing a model of effective behaviour which the learning manager can imitate
- Coaching the manager by suggesting or demonstrating alternative approaches or techniques
- Risk sharing with the manager by accepting some responsibility for the results of learning or by engaging in a similar learning activity at the same time.

Each of these processes can be undertaken by boss, adviser, subordinates, or colleagues. It is, of course, the boss who in managerial theory has the greatest responsibility for developing his subordinates and who therefore should, in theory, be providing help under each of these headings. I believe that, in fact, many bosses have been given a responsibility which they are quite unable to sustain in practice, and will remain unable to sustain however much their theoretical responsibility is emphasized in management development literature or in the bureaucractic requirements of management development schemes. It is, in my view, much more helpful for the learning manager to recognize the kind of help he may get from his boss than to try and establish a plaster image of what a good development boss would be and then regret how few bosses actually match the image.

Roles for the boss in helping managers to learn

I am not saying that the boss is not a crucial factor in helping managers to learn. I am saying that recent literature on coaching by the boss has given many bosses a role so intolerable that it is not surprising that few of them attempt it. Because of the theoretical primacy of the boss in learning, I will deal with his contributions now before turning to the role of the learner's colleagues.

The boss as provider and organizer of learning

Chapter 3 emphasized what the manager could do to analyse his own learning needs, and chapter 6 discussed why many bosses do not contribute as fully as they should to the identification and implementation of learning opportunities for their subordinates, I will not, therefore, repeat those comments on the boss as provider of learning opportunities, but add to them.

In this chapter we are concerned with how real time opportunities are tackled once the need and opportunity have been identified. Clearly, if the boss has himself contributed to either identification of need or identification of opportunity, he is more likely to be aware of the kind of contribution he can make to the learning process. One kind of help is actually to discuss with the learning manager what the nature of the learning opportunity is, to stimulate and supplement the learner's thoughts about what can be learned and how it can be learned. I have used the verbs 'stimulate' and 'supplement' deliberately, because a boss who attempts to 'direct' the learning of one of his subordinates is unlikely to achieve much unless his direction coincides with what the learner is committed to achieve by his own internal motivation, or by other external pressures.

The most useful thing the boss can do as organizer of learning is to encourage the learner to think about the learning process, and particularly about what he is trying to achieve. He can encourage a planned approach both to opportunities and to the learning process and he can encourage a reflective reviewing of experience. In short, he can assist the learner to organize his learning.

While this process is not carried out as well as it could be by many bosses, there is no inherent or complex reasons for failure to carry out this managerial role.

The boss as part of the learning environment

We have looked earlier at some aspects of the boss as part of the environment for the learning manager. He can be encouraging or dismissive in his attitude to learning needs and opportunities, particularly in relation to priorities. While the sudden withdrawal of a manager from a course because of a decision by his boss is a common and easily recognized phenomenon, bosses' attitudes to learning from opportunities on the job can be either positive or negative. They may be not only puzzled by an attempt to get both learning and task achievements out of one activity, but feel that performance is threatened by it. Certainly, their attitude to the risks taken by a manager who is prepared both to recognize his own weaknesses, and to experiment—and perhaps fail—in an attempt to learn how to remedy them, can be crucial.

Quite often, the short-term interests of the boss for immediate performance are in conflict with the longer-term possibilities and needs for learning of his subordinates. I have argued earlier that, for this among other reasons, the learning manager should not rely on the boss as being a favourable element in the environment, with the learner's interests at heart. However, when the boss positively enhances the learning environment, additional learning will flow (see chapter 4).

The boss as monitor of learning achievement

The boss is normally required by the organization to monitor and report on the extent to which his subordinates have improved their performance on any activities on which he may earlier have reported weaknesses. The reports are usually part of a formal appraisal, and typically talk more about changes in terms of results achieved rather than in terms of learning. This is reasonable enough, since what needs to be learned will probably not have been specified very clearly. Also, in practice, bosses are more likely to be concerned about results rather than about the learning necessary to achieve results. Finally, he is likely to be only partially knowledgeable about either the learning objectives or the learning results, since both of these are often the internal property of the learner.

The boss is therefore normally not required by the organization to take a serious role as monitor of learning effectiveness. Where he is knowledgeable about what the learner is trying to achieve—for example, on a task force or special project—then his monitoring role is both important and feasible. The boss can, of course, also monitor learning in the sense of being present and observing the learning process—for example, seeing how a subordinate experiments with a new style of dealing with a difficult shop steward, or how he responds to an inquisition on a project behind schedule. Where he is in some sense sharing the learning experience, he is really acting the role of coach, to which I turn later.

The boss as provider of feedback

The boss is in a potentially powerful position to provide feedback to the learner on the results of his attempts to put learning into practice. Because of his position of power and authority, anything he says about the performance of his subordinates could be influential in reinforcing or denying the effectiveness of what the subordinate has learned. There are, however, serious problems for the learner in securing useful feedback.

Unless the boss has been associated with the learner in setting learning goals, it is unlikely that feedback will actually help to improve performance. General feedback, not associated with agreed goals, is not well received. To be effective, feedback has to be related to the job and to the subordinate; otherwise it may create resentment, hostility, and reduced performance (Carroll and Tosi[1]). Casual feedback on an *ad hoc* basis is not usually helpful, because it tends to be presented without sufficient thought for the sensitivities and likely reactions of the recipient. Unfortunately, most bosses are better at describing what they thought went wrong, and give higher priority to this, than they are at helping managers to see exactly what happened. Feedback tends to consist of generalizations ('You antagonized him', 'Your introduction was too long', 'You took too long to come to the point'). While such statements seem reasonable enough to those who make them, they usually create a barrier of defensiveness in the recipient. They also tend to create within the recipient the 'you-too' response ('Look who's telling me that I lack sensitivity').

Another general problem with providing useful feedback is magnified by the boss–subordinate relationship, particularly by fears on the part of the subordinate about the purpose of the feedback. This problem is, again, that bosses are more interested in end results than in the processes by which the results are achieved, yet it is the detailed processes which are useful in learning terms. It would be desirable for bosses to give feedback in more specific behavioural terms:

'Do you know how many times you interrupted X?'
'I made a note of your reactions to Y's proposals; do you know that you gave an encouraging response once, but five times you made negative replies?'

I have argued the case for specific behavioural data of this kind earlier in the book. However, with their many other concerns and priorities, it is not surprising to me that bosses do not, and in fact cannot, give this kind of analytical attention to the work of their subordinates.

Another problem with feedback from the boss is that there are inevitably limitations on how specific and accurate his feedback can be. He does not see all that his subordinate does; he sees a part directly, but the other part he sees only second-hand, through results. As an example, it is very difficult for bosses to get a direct picture of a manager's relationships with his colleagues.

The learning manager needs to recognize and learn how to deal with these problems of feedback from his boss, which seem to me to arise inevitably from the reality of the job of the boss. Although I will be setting out ways later of securing feedback from other sources, I am not suggesting that the learning manager can or should avoid getting feedback from his boss. What he should do is try to turn what may initially be poor feedback to advantage. One way of doing this is to engage with the boss in a process of planning the feedback in advance, so that instead of being faced with unplanned, *ad hoc* comments, the learner agrees with his boss specific areas in which the boss will watch and comment. Another appropriate technique is for the learner to avoid the almost inevitable defensive response to criticism ('It wasn't really like that', or 'So what would you have done?', neither of which really provides learning at this stage). Instead, the boss can be asked to produce some more data ('What did A do which made you think I had antagonized him?', 'Did you happen to make a note of how long the introduction took?').

The boss as model

I mentioned modelling in chapter 4 as one of the most powerful learning processes. As Handy pointed out: 'The conscientious developer of men will often be less successful in training good subordinates than the manager who spends no formal time on such activities'—if the latter is seen as a desirable model. The kind of imitative actions familiar to us from observing children model their behaviour on that of their parents are present in a somewhat enhanced, and usually less physical, form with managers. Managers can model their behaviour on a number of other factors, so the role of the boss as model is not unique. They model their boss following observation of him, or following mutual participation on a management task.

The ways managers model their behaviour on that of their boss can be seen on a bi-polar axis (see Fig. 8.1). They do it consciously or unconsciously, and

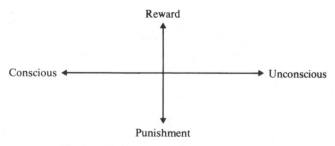

Fig. 8.1. The boss as the manager's model

135

they do it because of the expectation of rewards (or 'positive reinforcement', in learning language) if they behave as their boss does, or of fear of punishment if they do not.

The first essential for the learning manager is to try to assess how far his actions are, in practice, being influenced by what he sees his boss doing. It is important to emphasize that modelling is mainly based on what the boss *does*, not on what he *says* he will do. Thus a manager may observe from the behaviour of his boss that all work done by subordinates should be checked in detail, and model his behaviour on that observation. He will not model his behaviour on what his boss says about delegation—except that he might also repeat the same phrases while behaving in a contradictory fashion.

A believer in behaviourist learning theory might want to argue from this example, while accepting the powerful role of modelling, that it does not really matter whether the process through which the modelling takes place is conscious or unconscious. I believe it does matter, and that the learning manager would benefit from working out what the basis of his modelled behaviour is. Since I have argued the importance of learning appropriate to particular situations, it seems to me crucial that the learner knows whether the reward or punishment reason is likely to operate in the next managerial situation. I have encountered a number of managers who took up behaviours which they did not actually think effective in order to avoid criticism from their then boss. Those who recognized why they had modelled their behaviour on their boss had a much easier accommodation with a subsequent boss than did those who had not recognized, or buried, the reason and therefore found it difficult to recognize the need to change to meet the new situation.

I have given what may be seen as rather negative examples first—of managers learning to do what is temporarily useful rather than really effective. Of course, modelling can be a wholly desirable process through which learners acquire behavioural habits likely to be of permanent value. A manager can model himself on boss behaviour likely to be valuable in most situations, such as always asking people to spell out their objectives, or asking subordinates what the options are before making a decision, or never going into a meeting without a view of what to get out of it.

Finally, I should mention the role of the boss as a negative model. Some managers have told me that the only contribution to their learning made by a particular boss was that he gave a good demonstration of what not to do, or how not to go about getting desirable results. As one put it to me: 'I saw how a clever man who insists on pushing his cleverness can antagonize other people; I thought I would try to be clever and subtle.' Another boss was described to me: 'He is full of fire and fury before we go into a meeting, and full of deference and easy agreement when we get there. We call him Weasel; I'm never going to give my staff the chance to call me that.'

Warner Burke[2] has suggested that one of the reasons for the special problems of women managers is that they do not have other women managers on whom they can model effective behaviour. Since I believe there are special problems in being a woman manager, this is an important point, even though somewhat of a chicken-and-egg argument. Burke argues that the women manager 'lacks female role models that clearly demonstrate it is possible to be both competent and female'.

There can be little doubt about the significance of the boss as model for learning. He is a major feature of the learner's environment, he has power to say 'be like me', either explicitly or implicitly, and he often demonstrates effectiveness in the way most revered by managers—by achieving desired results. He probably is not conscious of how strong a model he is to his subordinates, and is unlikely to use himself deliberately as a model for consciously designed learning purposes. If he analysed his own behaviour for its potential impact on learning, he would in all probability find himself confused by his two roles. He may believe that his own behaviour is pretty effective and therefore have no wish to alter it with possibly detrimental effects on task achievement. It may also be his view that it would be difficult substantially to change or modify his behaviour, and particularly difficult to do so in order to provide a theoretically more appropriate model.

What the learning manager does, therefore, is to increase his conscious awareness of what his boss is doing, and what happens as a result of his doing it—the reactions of others, the relationship between objectives, actions, and results. He can then choose to model himself on positively advantageous learning rather than temporarily attractive avoidance of pain.

The boss as coach

There is no denying the actual direct influence of many bosses on learning by their subordinates. In the early 'seventies increased attention to on-the-job experiences as a major part of manager development led logically, naturally, and properly to emphasis on the role of boss as coach. The term 'coach' carries with it some inappropriate associations with the kind of technical training offered by sporting coaches, but the new movement in fact tended to give less significance to the role of the boss as a sort of one-to-one tutor and more to his role as a kind of Father Confessor, acting as a relatively uninvolved, objective counsellor, helping his subordinates recognize and deal with their own imperfections, and also helping them to reflect on and analyse (i.e., learn from) their experiences.

This latter coaching role for the boss has two problems. First, it attacks the priorities for use of their time given by most bosses who would see no significant return to them from the time spent coaching. Second, it asks managers to operate in a style which is foreign to many of them; bosses quite often are successful because they have the ability to be decisive and to get others to operate basically in the way they (the bosses) want them to operate. Their approach is naturally to judge and reach conclusions. The non-judgemental, sharing, non-directive, reflective relationship most frequently advocated recently for the manager as coach can be operated effectively. Some managers tend to work that way naturally in other parts of their managerial life, others have acquired a range of behavioural flexibility which enables them to behave as a non-directive coach one day, and as authoritative fire-fighting executive the next. My observation of managers at work tells me that the two categories together are in a minority. I have argued that, instead of trying to force all managers into a coaching role, we should help and encourage those whose basic managerial style is appropriate for an effective coaching relationship with learners.[3] I did not include in the article cited the possibility of an authoritarian boss being an effective coach in the old-fashioned, one-to-one instruction sense. The problem here is that the learner now has a role conflict, since by and large even junior and inexperienced managers do not like being given instruction. There are occasions, however, when coaching in a directive form is both appropriate and acceptable. A boss may be very well equipped to tell a subordinate what has happened in the past and to illustrate its relevance to a current event. He can listen to a rehearsal of an important presentation and comment on it. He can go over a written report and show how omissions or relative emphases may affect the reception of the report. He can tell a subordinate the reasons for differences in a similar product sold by his company in Florida, USA, and Dagenham, England.

The boss as coach can therefore offer coaching in two roles. He will be most familiar with, and probably happiest with, coaching in the form I have just illustrated. He will in all probability be less familiar and less happy with the style of coaching which operates through causing a manager to recognize and operate on his own weaknesses, and helping him to reflect on and analyse his experience. The really fortunate learning manager has a boss who is good at both and uses both styles appropriately. A less fortunate but sometimes almost equally effective learning manager has a boss who is good in one style but not the other, recognizes what his boss is good at, and optimizes his learning opportunities from that style. In neither situation should the learning manager believe that coaching is necessarily something offered primarily or most effectively by his boss; the alternative sources of coaching are discussed later in the chapter.

The boss as risk sharer

We looked in chapter 5 at the significance of the element of risk involved in learning. To be an effective aid in the learning process, the boss has to accept some risks. One kind of risk is that involved in allowing a subordinate to undertake a task or assignment for which he is not fully equipped but from which he will learn, perhaps at the expense of immediate results. Bosses are more prepared to make allowance for failure in retrospect than they are to accept the risk of failure as a prospect. Another kind of risk is that a manager who has learned will want to practise what he has learned, and may push for more opportunities or for a different job, inconveniently for the boss. A further risk is that the learning manager will become more effective than his boss.

All these are risks arising from the attempts of the manager to learn; the boss who accepts them will be giving one kind of help. There is another kind of help he can offer, by taking the risk of exposing himself and his own needs, and perhaps going further and participating in a shared learning experience. These are really the most dangerous risks for the boss, but may well be particularly influential in helping managers to learn. Examples of the first of these processes are seen when a boss says that he is uncertain how to handle a particular situation, or feels that a decision of his has not turned out well; the boss is widening the experience of his subordinate, and also demonstrating the significance to the boss of attempts to learn from experience. Participation in a shared learning experience could occur through a discussion of these problems, or could be achieved by thinking ahead to an event in which they would both be involved: 'This is the first time either of us has been involved in negotiating in the Middle East; let's both keep notes on what happens and see what we have learned at the end of the day.'

It is entirely understandable that many bosses are unwilling to face some of the risks involved to them in their subordinates' learning. The learning manager tries to work out which risks are acceptable, and works out a strategy to make use of the situations in which his boss will take a risk and avoid those where he will not. Perhaps most of all, he needs to help his boss accept risks by being prepared to analyse honestly his failures, showing what he has learned from them rather than attempting to deny or conceal his failures and therefore losing the opportunity to check what he has learned.

The boss as mentor

The unique role for the boss, one that cannot really be carried out by anyone else, is that of mentor. The boss who takes a personal interest in the career of another person, who becomes involved with him as a person, who provides opportunities to learn and to talk about learning, is acting as mentor for that person. From the point of view of the learning manager, the problem is that this is a role which can only really be offered, not sought. The learning manager can look for a boss who is going to help him develop, but he cannot search for someone with whom he is going to have the special relationship implied in the word 'mentor'. I have encountered few examples of genuine mentors, but those I have seen have offered something special to both parties. An article by Roche[4] reported that two thirds of executives thought they had had a mentor, but his definition of mentor embraced anyone who took a personal interest in another person's career. This seems to me too broad a definition, as I believe only someone with close personal commitment to someone else deserves the description mentor. It is not a role which standard management development schemes can include, because it does frankly include elements of favouritism. It is rather like the habit of bees who give a future queen special jelly in order to prepare her for her destiny, a favour not always returned in later life by the queen, who may have been an unworthy recipient.

Some of the special features of the mentor relationship (and, in my view, some of its weaknesses) are revealed in another *Harvard Business Review* article.[5] It is interesting that, in the companies discussed, the personal mentor relationship was extended into a sponsor relationship where the guiding hand was no longer that of the boss, showing how a successful learning process can be extended beyond its original boundaries.

The boss as an aid to learning

It seems to me pointless to press bosses to undertake roles in relation to their learning subordinates which cause internal conflict and demand skills which managers often do not possess.

It is not very useful to press a boss into personally providing learning opportunities which are foreign to his own preferred style—for example, to ask him to encourage reflective learning when he is himself largely an active experimenter. It is even less useful when to do so causes unfulfilled expectations in learners, creating dissatisfactions needlessly. While undoubtedly many bosses could do more within the limitations of their own skills and attitudes than they do, the learning manager is best advised to establish what the opportunities for learning from his boss really are, and to look to supplement them from other sources—which may, in fact, work more effectively anyway.

Learning through colleagues

In looking at the ways in which the boss can help, we have used headings which also fit the ways in which the learning manager's colleagues can help. Whereas, however, many bosses will feel a responsibility to help in one or more of the ways I have suggested, but may not do it very well, colleagues rarely feel a responsibility, but can often help more effectively than the boss. The initiative is necessarily, therefore, more with the learning manager, and in this section I will both describe ways in which they can help and ways in which the learning manager can ask for help.

Helping to organize learning opportunities

Just as the boss can help a manager recognize and take advantage of opportunities to learn, so the manager's colleagues can assist him. They will have little to do with the identification of assignments and committees, but can be much more helpful in suggesting ideas about how a colleague can learn from an experience that a boss may have been influential in obtaining. They may be able to describe how they set about learning from similar experiences; they may be able to indicate what is actually available to learn ('When I was appointed to lead Project 2000, I decided that I could really fill in my financial knowledge if I had a session for half an hour each week with the management accountant').

Colleagues can be helpful not only in identifying opportunities to learn, but in suggesting different methods of learning, and different styles of learning. A manager who has never been particularly conscious of how he has learned could certainly be intrigued (and may be helped) by being exposed to a manager whose characteristic style of learning is not just to experience but to reflect on his experience.

The role of colleagues in helping a manager to organize his learning in the sense of helping him to establish what his learning needs are introduces more difficult relationship problems than the suggestions made above. There are managers who would be able to share the confidences involved in discussing with a colleague what his strengths and weaknesses are, but in most cases business relationships do not allow this kind of exchange to take place. The learning manager could, however, look out for colleagues with whom he would not be inhibited. The colleague might be one with whom he has no strong working relationship which could affect the discussion, or one who is in no sense a competitor for preferment, or one who is known to be analytical and objective in his views of other people.

Managers may be offered opportunities to learn by colleagues in a way which is scarcely 'organized'. An invitation to visit a plant or go on a trip to see an important customer is quite likely actually to be seen as a learning opportunity, but may be unplanned, arising from a spontaneous conjunction of an occasion and a person.

Colleagues and the environment for learning

While the boss is often the most crucial factor in the environment in terms of his attitude to learning, the attitude of a manager's colleagues is also highly significant. If they are themselves also trying to learn, colleagues, like bosses, offer rewards and punishments to managers who try to learn, but both reward and punishment tend to be less direct. There will, perhaps, be a degree of mutual support and encouragement. If they are not trying to learn, or are unsympathetic to the needs of a colleague or to the ways in which he sets about trying to learn, then the environment may be at best neutral and at worst antagonistic.

On the whole, I find that managers are more worried about what their colleagues' attitudes to learning might be than they are experienced in what these attitudes actually are. However, the effective learning manager certainly will think about this issue and not propose learning experiences for himself which are wholly out of key with the support he may receive from the environment.

Colleagues monitoring learning

The extent to which a colleague can monitor someone else's learning is clearly related to how far he knows what the manager is trying to learn. He is only likely to know if the manager has shared with him, at least to some extent, his problems, learning needs, and learning objectives. This kind of sharing is infrequent because managers are not usually encouraged to undertake it, and because—as we saw on the issue of organizing opportunities—there are issues of risk involved in sharing knowledge of your weaknesses with others.

Paradoxically, it is far less risky in most circumstances to share this knowledge with a selected colleague than with your boss. Of course, the colleague has to be carefully chosen as someone who has the ability to monitor what the learning manager is trying to achieve, the skills of giving useful feedback (which I will describe later), and the intention of keeping confidential the information he acquires as a result of monitoring. Within these boundaries, colleagues are often in a better position to monitor than is a boss, because they may see the manager perform more often and because the reasons why they are monitoring are not confused by the needs of the boss to evaluate performance as a boss rather than as a helper of learning.

The kind of things which a colleague can monitor include:

- What the manager actually does during a meeting or discussion ('I am going to try to be less dominating in this discussion. Will you keep an eye on how successful I am?'. 'I am going to try and get him to state his objectives clearly without doing it for him'.)
- The reactions of others to his behaviour ('Jack is generally silent at these meetings and I want to bring him out. Tell me what he does when I try this at our next meeting'.)
- Whether a piece of new information has been effectively used ('You know that financial figures are not my strong point, but at the next budget meeting I am using DCF for the first time. Let me know afterwards if I made errors.')
- The level of skill employed ('I want you to make notes on my presentation—not the content but the style—and tell me how I could have done better.')

As I have pointed out earlier in the chapter, good planning will improve monitoring simply by causing it to be more specific and more clearly related to actual learning needs rather than to curiosity.

Colleagues providing feedback

The point of asking a colleague to monitor is obviously not to contribute to a thesis on managerial behaviour, but to acquire relevant and valid information. Unless the information is relevant (to the manager's learning needs) and valid (not just accidental or related to a unique, unrepeatable situation), there is no chance of it actually being useful. As I have just said in relation to monitoring, mutual planning of what is to be studied is desirable as a means of acquiring relevant and valid data.

It is also necessary to repeat two points about feedback made elsewhere in this book. Feedback has to be given in specific terms, and preferably should be given about behaviour rather than about attitudes. The general point about the motivation to learn is also important here: unless the learner is interested in the particular point on which feedback is being given, it is unlikely that feedback will help learning—at best, it may help to create conditions in which a manager is motivated to want to learn on that particular issue. Quite often, however, feedback fails to achieve anything because it is addressed to a need recognized by the person giving the feedback but not by the manager receiving it.

To give feedback in specific terms rather than in general descriptions is not easy as a controlled process (rather than as an occasional outburst related more to emotions than to learning needs). The single item of feedback I have heard quoted most often is 'I have told X that his relationships with Y need to be improved.' As I showed in chapter 3, this kind of feedback creates defensiveness, bewilderment, and frustration. More useful feedback addresses itself to specifics, where those specifics are part of a general pattern. Which aspect of his relationship with Y? 'I noticed that you disagreed with Y seven times in 45 minutes, and he with you five times.'

This last illustration serves also to repeat the point I made in chapter 3—that it is more useful to deal with behaviour rather than attitudes in feedback. More often than not, attempts to give feedback on attitudes leads to a flat denial by one or more of the parties involved ('You are wrong to say I am contemptuous of him; I have a lot of respect for his experience'). Dealing in specific behaviours is either less arguable or at least gets argument on to more useful ground. Instead of saying 'You look down on your colleagues', it is more useful to give feedback on the number of times a manager has expressed his own view, the number of times he has given credit to the views of others, the number of times he has supported the proposals of others.

The point about feedback being related to the learner's existing motivation to learn may seem a contentious one. My emphasis is, however, on the objective of the feedback . If the objective of the feedback is to make someone more aware of his learning needs, this ought to be part of the 'contract' between the learning manager and the colleague he has asked to help. If it is part of the contract, it may help him to recognize a learning need rather than creating defensiveness. If general feedback is not part of the contract, it is better to concentrate on those things on which feedback has been requested, as shown by the examples given in the Monitoring section. Enthusiastic feedback on sensitive subjects which the manager does not, in fact, want to discuss tends to lead to an end to requests for feedback.

The great advantage of feedback from carefully selected colleagues is that it can be sought and given in a learning context instead of in an evaluative context as it must be with the boss. Colleagues are less dominated by thoughts like 'Can I really let him handle this?' 'Is he good enough for this job?' 'Does this show he is not ready for promotion?' I am not claiming that these questions do not arise in the minds of colleagues, but I am sure that they are less obtrusive, and therefore less damaging to effective feedback.

Colleagues providing a model

I heard on the radio one day a sad story about a chaffinch which seemed to me a very apt one about modelling. A chaffinch brought up without hearing other chaffinches sing gave a flat, impoverished version of singing compared with the richness of others; it lacked anything on which to base its attempts. Of course, managers are not brought up in isolation from other managers, but they can be brought up without seeing examples of some of the good practices which it would be sensible to model themselves on—and they can also see some managers who sing some songs rather badly.

Modelling on colleagues is essentially no different from the process of modelling on the boss I have already described. There are the same issues of conscious and unconscious modelling, the same possibilities of modelling positively features recognized to be advantageous, or deciding not to do things in a certain way because of the negative results observed. Perhaps the biggest advantages of modelling on colleagues are that there are likely to be (because of the numbers involved) more desirable features to observe and model, and that there is less likelihood of a direct relationship of reward or punishment in connection with the behaviour modelled. This later point may well be modified with particular colleagues who may reward or punish particular forms of behaviour, but more in an interpersonal than in a managerial sense.

Just as with modelling on the boss, the prime concern for the learning manager ought to be that he is aware of and then makes use of the opportunities to model his behaviour on the effective practices of others. This means that he needs to be able to observe and analyse what is making the behaviour of others effective or ineffective. In addition, it would be useful if he could discuss with receptive colleagues exactly what it is that they do as they perform effectively. Some may not know, but others will be able to describe the processes through which they go. At this point, the learning manager is probably receiving coaching, and having made the point now that these processes—monitoring, receiving feedback, modelling, coaching—are not necessarily in separate compartments, I will leave further discussion of coaching for the next section.

Although it is clear that a great deal of individual behaviour is built up through modelling, not all that much is known about how it actually happens. From a deliberate learning point of view, I have emphasized planning, analysis, and reflection, and I think many managers are capable of doing more of this even if it is not their natural learning style. With many managers, it may be a less considered, less conscious form of behaviour, and I find it tends to arise most frequently when a manager has a general admiration for a colleague, from whom he then picks up certain forms of behaviour which he feels to be congruent with his own. It is less frequent for managers to model particular forms of behaviour on colleagues whom they do not in general admire. While I think it would in fact be valuable if managers were able to extend their learning flexibly to this latter form, there are considerable barriers to overcome. I have found that the barriers caused more problems than the attempt to overcome them is worth.

I have already referred several times to the virtues of studying behaviour specifically and analytically; since the ways of doing this relate to many different real time learning processes, I have included a separate section on this at the end of this chapter.

Colleagues providing coaching

I have discussed the problem of the boss in meeting the theoretical require-ments on him to act as coach. Many of these problems are diminished for a colleague acting as coach. Perhaps most important of all, a colleague acting as coach is normally doing so at the personal request of the manager who wants to learn. (If he has, in fact, been forced on the learning manager by the latter's boss, then real learning is difficult to achieve.) Other advantages of using colleagues as coaches include the greater variety of expertise available, the reduced risks to the learner, the increased number of occasions on which coaching can be sought, and clarity that learning and not performance is the main concern.

There are, however, still the issues of risk and status referred to on monitor-ing and receiving feedback, so the sensible learning manager will seek those colleagues who will not damage his credibility. Some colleagues will be significantly flattered by the approach, since it clearly reflects well on them.

When I described the role of the boss as coach, I discussed the extremes of coaching behaviour, from the attempt to transfer information from an expert, to the non-directive, reflective style which is intended to help the manager learn more from his own efforts. Colleagues can be used in exactly the same ways, and may suffer from the same misapprehensions about what effective coaching is. It is for the learning manager to make up his own mind about the kind of coaching help he wants and then to specify it to his colleague.

Here are some examples of coaching by colleagues:

A production manager had worked his way up the organization entirely on the production side, having left school at sixteen. In his early thirties, he met and found he could talk comfortably with a marketing manager who was different in education and experience. They had one or two clashes in meetings, after which he said to the marketing manager: 'You seem to know more about my problems on production than I do about yours on marketing.

I would like you to go over the agenda for our weekly management meeting with you, so you can explain to me what is involved from a marketing point of view. For example, you keep pressing me to make arrangments for preferred customers, and I don't really understand what the marketing reason for that is'.

A manager found when he took over as departmental manager that there were a number of new reports on financial issues which he found it difficult to understand. His attempts to get his own financial managers to explain the reports were unsuccessful, so he decided to call for help from a financial colleague from a different part of the company, whom he had met on a course. His specification to his colleague was : 'I don't want you to tell me what they mean, I want you to listen while I tell you what I think they mean, and then you tell me where I've got it wrong.'

A manager had received comments from his boss that he was creating unnecessary antagonisms by his behaviour at their weekly management meeting. The manager felt that, although there was truth in this, his boss was too concerned to have a comfortable time, was not interested in difficult issues, and was therefore simply trying to shut him up. He sought out one of his colleagues who he thought had shown some sympathy for his attempt to raise problems. He asked him to analyse his attempts to raise the issues, give him feedback about how he had gone about it, and give him ideas on how he could raise the same issues in ways which would not create antagonism.

A newly appointed manager found that the week was too short to deal with the problems which came into his office. He was particularly concerned about whether he was dealing with the really important issues. He had a senior experienced manager as a subordinate, and arranged to have a regular half-hour meeting with him on Monday morning: 'Help me decide what is really important this week.'

This last illustration brings out a form of colleague help which many managers find particularly difficult: getting assistance from subordinates. The reason is partly that managers do not think of the possibility of learning from subordinates. If they are more expert than the manager, this is usually seen by him as something to control and to hide rather than to acknowledge openly, even to himself. Even if managers can be brought to recognize that there are things on which subordinates could help them, there are barriers of status and technique for both of them which make it very difficult in practice, and I have found few managers who are able to face both the possibility and the problems; usually they will turn sideways to get similar help from someone who is not a subordinate. That is why I have included the particular example, because it seems to me that a manager will, in fact, only be able to use a subordinate as a coach in special circumstances of age or non-competitiveness, where the man may appear more as a colleague than as a subordinate.

I pointed out earlier that it was very difficult for boss and subordinate to agree to risk learning together. The same considerations have much less application between colleagues.

There are basically two ways in which colleagues can share learning risks. They can explicitly set about learning the same kind of things from shared experiences—both can, for example, agree to engage in the same kind of experimenting behaviour and compare notes about the results. Alternatively, they can agree to help each other to learn from different experiences or different aspects of the same experience. An example of this latter kind of sharing would be that, having exchanged learning goals with each other, they analyse and discuss the experiences from which they think they have learned. They are sharing both the risk of revealing an original weakness and that of revealing that their attempts to learn in relation to it have not been fully effective. Examples of this include the following cases:

> A manager had a colleague who had the reputation of being a first-class report writer; when he went to him and asked if he would look over an important report he had just drafted, he found that his colleague wanted a 'trade'. The good report writer was much less effective in chairing meetings, and asked for comments and advice on that.

> A manager was nominated to represent his organization on an external committee, and found it very difficult to decide how to conduct himself with other people who were mainly much senior to him. He talked with a friend outside his organization who attended a different trade association and got ideas from him. His friend wanted help too; he was for the first time dealing with unionized representations of supervisory staff and wanted to discuss problems with him.

Learning from colleagues—a general summary

One of the lasting contributions of the organization development movement has been to provide improved understanding of, and better mechanisms for resolving, the issues of interpersonal and interdepartmental conflict. As a result, although I know of no research specifically on the subject, I believe we can see why managers do not recognize and do not utilize opportunities to learn from each other. The OD movement has given us some tools for tackling the issues of openness, trust, and confidence on a large scale. On the specific issue of learning, the same requirements obtain. It is unlikely that a manager who tries to conceal his learning needs from a colleague from whom he wants learning help will be successful in learning. Not all managers are able to offer their needs openly, and not all their colleagues will be able to respond with equivalent openness. Some managers will only be able, therefore, to use the modelling opportunity offered by their colleagues, but others will be able to ask for and receive more. It is their choice how far they want to go, and their choice of which colleague will give suitable help.

Learning through a personal diary

As I showed in chapter 5, managers tend to be active experimenters rather than reflective observers in their learning style. I have also said that learning is essentially a social, not a solitary, process. However, some managers are more introspective and more reflective than the average. For them, a diary can provide a useful learning tool. Chapter 3 described the use of a special form of diary-keeping as a means of establishing the facts about a manager's use of time. The point of this kind of diary is to be quantitative and analytical, rather than qualitative. This section is concerned with a diary which is more subjective, working through narration rather than predetermined charts—essentially, in fact, the kind of diary which many people have kept for at least a period of their life, in which they confide their personal thoughts and opinions.

As far as published information is concerned, we have to rely on analogies rather than actual examples of a manager's diary in this form. In Britain, the most dramatic illustration has been the diaries of Richard Crossman.[6] They are not an exact analogy, but they illustrate usefully the process of setting down what has occurred, more or less at the time it occurred, and—even more usefully—the value of occasionally sitting down to summarize what the diarist thinks he has learned. Thus, on 3 January 1965, Crossman set down his views on his civil servants, the cabinet, his senior colleagues, and the Prime Minister. Not flattering views, but views which affected his dealings with them. His civil servants, for example, were characterized as lacking 'any kind of constructive apprehension of the problems with which they deal and any kind of imagination'.

Of course, many well known diaries, from Pepys onwards, can be seen as documenting a learning process in the simple sense of recording information acquired. Crossman's diary is a more useful document for managers, in the sense that it illustrates a different kind of learning more appropriate to them. It describes how particular parts of the government process seem to work, it illustrates the skills of some of his colleagues (including some for whom he had no admiration in general), it talks about his relationship with his boss, the Prime Minister.

Crossman's reasons for writing his diaries were different from those which obtain with managers, who are unlikely to want to publish their own diaries. There is a certain amount of relief involved in the process of writing, perhaps expressing anger and frustrations which had to be concealed at the time (and also, perhaps, elements of self-deception as situations are replayed and written to the advantage of the diarist). Clearly, I am not arguing here that a manager should keep a diary for therapeutic purposes, but for learning benefits. To obtain these benefits, a manager must above all be honest with himself, and can perhaps more easily afford to be so if, unlike politicians, his diary is not to form part of a potentially publishable record. Writing a diary captures a version of the past, and if written for learning purposes it can sharpen and clarify recollection of what occurred.

For learning purposes, the manager's diary need not be an every-day or even an every-week commitment, although for a really well disciplined manager it could usefully be so. More managers would probably cope with the workload better if they undertook it as I do, after some particularly significant event. If they then record what happened, with particular reference to their own actions or to those of other people (behaviours again, not attitudes), they can then use the diary to work out possible reasons for what has occurred, alternative courses of action which might have been taken or which could be taken in the future. Although I have said the diary must be an honest record, written to aid learning rather than to sustain the ego, it does not have to be the equivalent of a confessional. Here is an example:

'For the third time I tried to get X to consider an alternative approach to the project he wants us to sponsor. First of all I asked him to set out the objectives more clearly, and to suggest different ways of meeting them. I got the objectives but only one approach. Then I asked him how we could justify the approach to finance, unless we gave alternatives. He came back with detailed costings and a statement that any alternatives would be more costly. I asked him what the alternatives were; he said it was not worth wasting time on paper exercises. I finally told him I wouldn't put the proposal up without options. He went away dissatisfied and I was annoyed. Clearly, I should have been more directive in the first place, instead of assuming he would work out for himself why alternatives are necessary'.

Observing and learning

I have referred to the opportunities available to the manager to learn for himself by observing others, and to learn from feedback resulting from others observing him. I have said that analysis and feedback can most helpfully be given in specific behavioural terms rather than in generalizations.

Much of the useful work dealing with observation has been done by Honey and Rackham in separate works to which I refer in chapters 3 and 10. Their work is concerned with more than the observation practices which I deal with here. In my own work involving observation of managers in action, I have confirmed for myself the impact of identifying and then using defined behaviour categories as a means of helping managers to learn how they behave, and then to measure their attempts to implement any changes they may decide on.

Useful as this work is, the problem for the manager is that he is unlikely to be trained as an observer, unlikely to have colleagues so trained, and unlikely to be one of the few managers able to call on the services of a specialist in observation. I have postponed until the final chapter ways in which managers can use specialist advisers in these and other ways, and in this section I will deal with analytical observation techniques only to the level at which I think an untrained manager has some chance of operating successfully on behalf of himself or others.

Some examples of specific behaviours have been given at various stages in this book, and it may be useful to draw together the points made so far about observing analytically.

- Observation must be based on categories which are discrete and not subject to varying interpretation
- It is done best if it is planned in advance
- It is most effective when it deals with behaviours rather than attitudes
- It is effective only in relation to purpose; observation in itself is only a form of visual gossip
- It will only be influential if it is related to a need recognized by the learner.

I want now to explain why managers who have not been trained in observation techniques should aim at a small number of behaviours rather than at a full range. The reasons is that observation for managers is a part-time occupation, not only in the sense that they are not specialists in it, but in the sense that they have to observe while participating. They should therefore concentrate on selected issues agreed by themselves, or by their learning colleague, as being especially important.

I will give only two examples here; more are given in the last chapter and in the books and articles referred to. I should emphasize that the categories of behaviour used have to be agreed by those who are going to use them. In my second example, the difference between 'building' and 'supporting' would need to be defined.

Analysis of selection interviewing

It is not infrequent for managers to conduct a selection interview with a colleague present—either another manager or a personnel specialist. Observation by one of the participants could be based on the following simple form of analysis:

Type of question	Number of occasions
Open	
Closed	
Leading	

Analysis of meeting behaviour

There is a vast range of behaviour which could be recorded at most meetings.

150

The illustration below followed a decision to concentrate on the specific items shown.

Contribution	Number of occasions		
	Brown	Green	White
Proposes action			
States difficulty			
Supports action			
Disagrees			
Builds on proposal			

It is probably necessary to repeat for managers who have not used this kind of approach why it is more useful as a learning tool than the more generalized form of observation and feedback many of us are familiar with. The first example shows specific behaviours which a manager can attempt to change, instead of him trying to grapple with a statement like 'I did not seem to be able to get him to talk'. The second illustration similarly highlights particular contributions, and also brings out the interactive nature of behaviour in meetings. 'Be more positive,' says the boss. The example shows what might be involved.

Planning and reflecting on learning experiences

I conclude this chapter by returning to the image of the self-directed learner specified in chapter 5. All the processes described in this chapter require a manager to put more thought into his learning processes. The suggestions made here give him a greater capacity to choose his own learning strategies and to control his own learning, instead of simply responding to the view of other people on what they will provide. If a manager cannot manage his own learning behaviour, how successful is he likely to be in attempting to manage the behaviour of others?

Questions

1. How far have you modelled part of your managerial behaviour on someone else?
2. Can you see some ways in which you could get more help on your learning needs from your boss?
3. Have you some colleagues from whom you could get useful help through, for example, feedback or coaching?
4. What opportunities are available to you for observing an effective colleague?

References

1. Carroll, S. J. and H. L. Tosi, *Management By Objectives—Applications and Research*, Macmillan, 1973.
2. Warner, Burke, 'Women in organizations' in *Current Issues in Organization Development*, Human Sciences Press, 1977.
3. Mumford, A. C., 'Management development—with or without the boss', *Personnel Management*, June 1975.
4. Roche, G. R., 'Much ado about mentors', *Harvard Business Review*, 1976.
5. Collins, E. G. C. and P. Scott (eds.), 'Everyone who makes it has a mentor', *Harvard Business Review*, July 1978.
6. Howard, A. (ed.), *The Crossman Diaries* Magnum Books, 1979.

9. Learning from courses

This chapter concentrates on what a manager needs to consider in order to choose to undertake a course, and how he can make most effective use of a course experience. The main emphasis is again on how a manager learns; there are few illustrations of the particular skills and knowledge that managers may acquire because these things are usually fairly well described in the course literature. The problem for the learning manager is not likely to be a fundamental disbelief in courses, but uncertainty about what kind of experience a course is, and lack of help in making best use of it.

Learning off the job, through courses or similar experiences, can be justified through a variety of arguments. I want to emphasize two points before I turn to the justifications for the creation of learning experiences off the job. The first is that it is common experience for a course to be treated as an isolated learning occasion, with very little close association with other learning experiences on the job; there is little real association, either in terms of content or method, despite references in course literature to 'learning about learning'. This lack of association is destructive of effective learning and unnecessary.

The second point is that few courses recognize in a coherent way the different learning styles likely to be represented among the managers attending the course; in so far as different methods of learning are offered during the course, this is more likely to be due to different styles in the tutorial staff, or to largely haphazard belief in the virtues of catholicity of method rather than to a coherent approach to the learning needs and styles of different managers. This situation, too, is unnecessary, and is a partial explanation of the failure of some courses to achieve the theoretical learning benefits which I will now describe.

A justification for courses

It is convenient to propose the one word 'course' to embrace similar learning events described as programmes, conferences, seminars, workshops. These description are often applied to managerial learning events, for prestige or marketing reasons.

The main justifications for courses are:

- The need to learn something quickly
- The greater learning effectiveness of situations designed as learning experiences, rather than situations focused on task achievement with subsidiary learning possibilities

153

- The failure to identify or make effective use of real time learning opportunities has led to the need to create alternative learning vehicles
- The desirability of learning in advance of the sometimes primitive experiences offered on the job
- The need for the acquisition of knowledge, information, or skill not available through current job experiences
- The opportunity to learn from a different group of people.

Steps in the learning process

The main steps in the learning process outlined in the previous chapter apply even more clearly to learning off the job:

- Collect data on what needs to be learned
- Set objectives for learning
- Define standards of performance
- Monitor achievement
- Review the reasons for deviation from standard
- Decide what additional action is necessary.

Unfortunately, these steps are rarely adequately defined with the learning manager, and insufficiently implemented with him. The process of collecting data on learning needs, setting objectives, and defining standards has been covered in earlier chapters (see chapters 3 and 8), so here I will concentrate on the last three steps.

Individual needs and courses

Courses are not designed to meet individual needs; they are an approximation to the needs (more or less well defined) of groups of managers. Even at their most specific, they can rarely be as appropriate to the needs of individual managers as the kind of real time processes described in the previous chapter. They may, however, be relatively effective because the learning process they employ is a process dedicated to learning rather than being an associated element to a task.

The process by which managers arrive on a course is often, as I showed earlier in the book casual, unanalytical, the result of environmental pressures ('We always send our best people to Harvard'). Chapter 3 gave ideas on the ways through which a manager could identify his own needs, and could as a result be interested in a course as a partial solution. This section will begin by reviewing the kind of solutions different types of course offer, and their relation to the learning styles of managers. I will subsequently try to give some help to the significant number of managers who find themselves committed to a course without the benefit of careful analysis of either their needs or the solution, indicating how they may none the less secure benefit from it.

Types of course

There is a bewilderingly large number of ways in which courses for managers can be divided:

In-company	—	External
Functional (e.g., marketing)	—	General (covering all functions)
Narrow status range	—	Broad status range
Concerned with skills (e.g., negotiating)	—	Concerned with concepts or environmental issues
Dealing with strategic issues	—	Dealing with operational issues
Aimed at immediate needs, task/role centred	—	Aimed at longer-term needs
High prestige, international	—	Low prestige, local

From the learning manager's point of view, the significance of these differences is how they relate to what he needs.

Unfortunately, course brochures are frequently sales documents and not really helpful in showing what will be provided, and how it will be provided. The learning manager therefore has to call on other forms of intermediate knowledge about particular courses, either from those who have attended, or from a personnel or management development adviser, or from an outside agency (such as the Management Courses Index in the UK). This is one area in which the genuinely self-directed learner shows himself by declining to accept the often vague, if well meant, assurances of others, and instead pursues these advisers or the course organizers about the specific relationship between what is expected to occur on the course and what he sees as his needs. He is then better able to identify what the course is likely to offer him.

The kinds of question which he can most usefully ask are a consequence of the kind of need he has. If a manager wants help on negotiating skills, will this particular course help with the particular skills he requires? Does it deal with negotiation in purchasing, or in industrial relations, or in professional relationships with undeveloped countries?

Similarly, when a manager's needs are though to be to acquire a better understanding of general management, is his need met by a course which gives a series of sessions on marketing, production, and finance in an attempt to improve his knowledge of departments in which he is not expert? Or would his needs be better met by a course which concentrates on the different role of a general manager as compared with the role of a functional manager? The answer depends on his needs, and only if he has analysed them can he assess the relevance of particular courses.

The learning manager is likely to have a hierarchy of needs, some of which may be met through a particular course and some not. Once he has satisfied himself that a course deals with an important need, he should prepare himself by thinking about the learning processes involved, his attitudes to them, and his own preferred style of learning.

I will describe first some of the processes which take place within a course.

Learning from tasks

The last two chapters were mainly concerned with how managers can be helped to learn from the experiences offered through work centred on the achievement of a task. The transition to learning through off-the-job processes explicitly designed as learning experiences is no longer as dramatic a change as it was seen as being ten or fifteen years ago. As we have already seen in looking at the approach adopted by Revans, a number of activities have been designed which, although specifically created as learning activities, are centred on the performance of a total management task. While the relative emphasis in a project on task or learning is likely to be important in terms of learning achievements, the actual nature of learning involved from doing a project 'to investigate and report on the distribution facilities of our companies in the UK' is not very different whether it is undertaken because the managing director wonders why empty lorries from several of his companies are passing each other on the motorway, or because the management development adviser has been looking for some useful projects for manager development.

Another reason for the blurring of the boundary between experiences provided as learning and experiences emerging from task responsibilities has been the adoption of task-centred activities within the most structured learning context—a course. Over the years, there has been an increase in the task-associated elements within many management courses. One early requirement was that a syndicate should report on its discussions on a management subject, thereby giving some practice in managerial tasks such as planning time, chairmanship, report writing, and oral presentation skills. To this kind of experience has been added a variety of activities which focus on performance of a task. I am distinguishing here first those aspects of a course where there is a task to carry out rather than simply a skill to exercise. The difference is illustrated by a course on interviewing skills, in which a manager is required to interview a fictional candidate for an invented job. Useful as this can be, the experience is designed to provide learning on a skill; there is no meaningful task except to interview well.

An example of task-centred activities is the kind of interactive business game played between competing 'companies' on a course. Such activities have a reality of their own, and are task centred in the sense that for many of the participants the point of the exercise is perceived to be that their company achieves the best results. Similar task-centred learning can be seen on courses where course members are given information on a company problem and are set the task of producing a report or presentation on it. Increased attention to behavioural skills in recent years has led to the design of various forms of exercise involving the creation of towers from children's building blocks, or paper planes. In the UK there has been some experiment in creating tasks focused on physical experiences, such as bridging a small ravine or climbing a cliff.

As I illustrated earlier, tasks designed to give practice in a particular skill, such as interviewing, also blur any attempt to define learning through courses as being in any simple sense totally different from learning through job experiences. Courses which deal with managerial skills such as decision making, chairing meetings, negotiating, would be unlikely nowadays to be considered useful if they did not include opportunities for course members actually to perform these tasks.

I have made these points about the strong task associations of at least some forms of management courses for two reasons. The first is that some managers do seem to put learning experiences in separate compartments, and fail to carry the kind of process which is employed to help them learn from task experiences on a course over to the similar experiences which they have in the task environment back on the job. The second reason is that I think that some of the emphasis on learning through tasks on courses has become misplaced. In some cases, performance of a task is seen as the only way of learning effectively, yet much less attention has been paid to ensuring that a manager is helped to learn than to creating ingenious exercises.

There has been a tendency to think that the provision of a task bearing some resemblance to real managerial life is not only likely to be attractive to the manager but that a manager will learn from the experience simply by being engaged in it. Although there is nowadays an increasing use of the phrase 'learning how to learn' in describing the purposes of management courses, I am not convinced that actual practice comes very close to this important objective.

If the course is not structured so as to incorporate the opportunity to review how learning from a task can be effectively achieved, and how to carry this learning about learning back onto the job, then the self-directed learner will set about creating his own opportunities to do this, in ways described later in the chapter.

Learning about skills

Undoubtedly, the most clearly demonstrable value of courses as structured learning experiences arises from those courses dedicated to helping managers to learn skills.

It will be useful to look at the reasons why courses are particularly effective in this area of learning. The first reason is that, assuming a manager has identified for himself or agreed that a particular skill needs to be improved or added to his repertoire, an activity specifically designed to illustrate effective use of the skill is attractive to him. The second reason is that the opportunity to experiment with the skill in a relatively well controlled environment, with helpful counsellors to comment on the way the skill has been implemented is one which is different from the normal real time experience (even if that experience includes elements of feedback and coaching, which is not always possible). Perhaps most crucially, learning a skill or improving a skill on a course is advantageous because it reduces the risks involved. The extent to which the risks are reduced depends on the particular situation of the course. If it is held in a 'stranger' environment, with no colleagues from the organization in which the manager works, then the problems of status and perceptions about manager performance are reduced (although still not entirely absent). If the course is held in company with colleagues, then the risks involved in experiment and achieved performance are more significant.

In either environment, the learning manager is the one who gives greater emphasis to the opportunities for learning offered than to the risks involved in demonstrating a degree of incompetence in the skill involved.

As the above comments have suggested, there are alternative courses which may be available to the learning manager. He may have a choice between a course on interviewing skills run by an external agency, or one run in-company. It is normally claimed that an in-company course will inevitably be more helpful to him because it will deal with examples which are specific to his situation. While it is true that in-company courses can be more directly related to the kind of problems he will face (although in large organizations even this may not be the case), it is also true that external courses on the same subject may be run more professionally, or with big 'names'. Perhaps more important than either of these is the fact that they can offer a level of anonymity which can be helpful to those managers who would otherwise be involved in problems of status and perceived performance on an internal course with lower-level colleagues. Essentially, the issue is one of which environment will provide the most suitable experience for the manager; this is partly a matter of learning content but partly a matter of his reaction to the environment.

There is now general agreement that in order to learn about skills a manager needs to be given:

- Some idea of the content of the skill involved
- The opportunity to practice the skill
- Help in reflecting on the results of his practice.

Of these, the opportunity to practice is widely agreed as the most essential. The days when managers listened to lectures or read articles or books about skills and had no opportunity to practise them are gone, certainly if the course is explicitly about a skill (some courses with more general objectives may give no opportunity for practice). Both skills exercised in one-to-one situations and skills exercised in groups can now be practised with direct feedback from video, thus providing the manager with the opportunity to study himself in action instead of relying solely on the comments of observers.

The types of skill in which managers may be helped will be familiar to managers who work for organizations which run internal courses or who frequently sponsor managers on external courses. Managerial skills may be more or less well defined, either at the 'needs' end or at the course end, so that there are still courses which presume to deal with a skill called 'leadership' (a skill largely related, in my view, to a particular environment), while other courses deal with skills more definable and less subject to particular situations. Examples of these latter include effective speaking, chairmanship, selection interviewing, decision making, negotiating.

There is also often thought to be a general skill of interpersonal relationships, although in fact this involves a number of separate diagnostic skills such as listening, analysing feedback, and then separate action skills such as proposing action, building on the proposals of others. These skills again seem to me often to be partly situational, in that while it is desirable for a manager to have these skills, particular situations may reward him for one and not the other. However, the best of these courses will aim to increase a manager's repertoire of behaviour rather than simply to press for the adoption of one kind of behaviour.

Learning facts

Managers often need facts before they can act effectively. In this section I am talking about objective information—for example, about matters of law or regulation, about what is meant by various forms of financial calculation, what company policy is on methods of dealing with customers or suppliers. Ways of learning these facts generally start with giving the manager the information to read; in a formally structured learning situation such as a course, he may be given the information orally or in writing or both. Some years ago, there was a vogue for putting information into specially tailored chunks of material ('programmed learning') either in books or in a cassette, the elements being very carefully designed for ease of assimilation and for checking that the information had been correctly acquired. Problems of flexibility and volume meant that this process has not really caught on, and for most managers learning facts is still dependent on reading or listening to information conveyed in the traditional form.

The virtue of programmed learning is that it is specifically designed to make it easy to learn, whereas normal books, articles, and lectures have a mixture of objectives which makes them less functional as instruments of learning.

In terms of the number of words passed per minute, reading would seem to be a much more effective learning process than listening. Yet managers are often more influenced by (and therefore learn more from) a lecture. Despite the research which shows an appalling retention rate following lectures, many managers prefer the human contact involved and, crucially, are influenced in their willingness to accept the information if their rating of the lecturer as a person/performer is high.

There is a high number of interacting variables on which method is most appropriate for learning facts. Managers often have a preference for a particular method, and claim that, for example, they always learn facts better from an article than a lecture. There is a considerable element of self-fulfilling prophecy about this. It seems clear that information which is highly complex is best conveyed (at least initially) in written form, whereas information which is less complex gains from the personal impact of a skilled lecturer.

As is the case with the whole subject of learning, it is unhelpful to see the learning of facts as an either/or situation, even at the stage of initial acquisition. A combination of reading, lecture, and interactive discussion is likely to be more effective for most people than a simple-minded decision in favour of one or the other. Equally, the use of some form of practice to reinforce the motivation to acquire facts and to add to conviction in using them is entirely desirable. A manager has not completed the learning process until he has put into practice what he has partially learned in the sense of acquiring facts.

An individual's view of course learning processes

Just as individual learning styles affect the extent to which real time learning opportunities are recognized and seized by the learning manager, so his style influences what he recognizes and uses of the learning opportunities available on a course. While I have met managers who claim never to have learned anything from any of the courses they have attended, I believe this to be an unusual condition, probably attributable to the relatively narrow range of learning styles favoured by many courses. Clearly, an active experimenter is unlikely to learn much from a course which provides him with information or concepts, but gives him no opportunity to experiment with applying the new information. Equally, a course which concentrates exclusively on providing opportunities to experiment with behaviour, without giving serious attention to the processes of reflection or conceptualization, will be a relatively ineffective learning experience for those whose learning style urges them in that direction.

It seems to me unlikely that most course designers really recognize the diversity of learning styles of managers. Where attempts have been made, they have either arisen from the different styles and interests of the course staff, or from a belief in the virtues of giving the learner responsibility for choosing his own approach to learning.

Since this book is aimed at managers rather than course designers, I am not going to tell designers how to design, but I am going to suggest how managers should identify and respond to the learning processes offered to them on courses.

My first suggestion is that managers should do what they can to identify in advance what kinds of experience will be made available on a course they are considering.

Course brochures are quite likely to describe the course content and list a variety of learning processes but less likely to indicate the balance between particular processes.

How much time in one room with all their course colleagues; how much time in small groups? How much time acquiring information from reading or lectures, how much time experimenting with individual skills? If a course is described as 'based on the case method', what does this mean? An attempt to have a serious dialogue on these issues in advance of the course should help the manager decide whether it is likely to be conducted in a way from which he is likely to learn.

Once on the course, discussion about the learning processes is affected by three factors. The course may be of that rare kind which actually provides time and encouragement for a discussion of what is actually happening in terms of learning (a discussion of group dynamics or interpersonal relationships is not the same thing). Even if course structure does not specifically encourage it, course staff may be interested to discuss with individuals what they are learning and how they are learning. Finally, the interests and style of the individual learner come into play; if he knows enough about himself and his own learning style to relate course processes to his style he may be able to analyse how far the processes used are actually helping him to learn and why. The process of analysing what is happening is, of course, particularly characteristic of the reflective observer, but need not be confined to him.

The manager I have described as the self-directed learner seeks to take responsibility for identifying his own learning needs and opportunities; in the same way, he will seek to look at learning processes on a course and his own response to them. If the course structure does not provide him formally with opportunities to reflect on an discuss these processes, he will take the initiative with course staff or colleagues. I have said that, although the process of looking at learning processes seems most characteristic of the reflective observer, it need not be confined to him. My reason for saying this is that a course is a specially designed learning event, providing special learning opportunities. Whatever the characteristics of a manager in his 'normal' real time learning mode, he can and should stretch that style to learn about himself and his learning style. One of the characteristics of courses is that they give people a chance to experiment with different styles of behaviour; it is particularly appropriate that one element of experiment should if necessary be with learning about learning.

Finally, the manager should take an opportunity after the course to reflect on the kind of learning experience it has been for him. Most managers nowadays would be asked to complete a report on a course of significant length, but most reports concentrate on what the manager wants to say about what he has learned, rather than how he has learned. Since the main point is for the manager to optimize his learning rather than to report on it, it is certainly more important for the manager to be encouraged to review for himself his own learning processes than to report on them so that others may benefit. The manager should therefore undertake an audit for his own purposes of the learning experiences offered on the course, and of how he responded to them. Again, this may seem characteristic of the reflective observer, but it is in fact something which can be undertaken by a manager who is normally more action oriented. Whereas the former may want to do it because he likes analysing experiences, the latter may do it in order to take action in the future. For him, the important questions are likely to be:

- What was my response to the different opportunities for learning (e.g., information collection, interactive behaviour, skill practice)?
- What have I learned from the way I responded?
- What could I do differently next time, faced with similar opportunities?
- How can I incorporate what I have learned about my learning style into how I learn from real time opportunities?

The self-directed learner is therefore someone who refuses to be a victim of what is offered to him on a course, either in content or in method, but makes a determined effort to manage his own response to what is offered.

Course learning processes—an academic model

I have deliberately described the individual's response to course learning processes first. Many course designers would have a different model of learning processes, in which they would start from generalizations about a relationship between what is to be taught and the most effective ways of learning. Thus, they would tend to relate the acquisition of knowledge to cognitive processes, usually dominated by formal instruction from a lecturer or book, whereas the development of skills would be identified with practical experimentation. I have given more emphasis to the style of the learner, not because the generalizations about the appropriateness of particular processes for particular objectives are invalid, but because in my view these generalizations have too often been overstated, in the sense that no equivalent concern for the interactions between the process and the individual learner's style has been shown. From the learning manager's point of view, the learning process on a course is set for him, and there is not much he can do about the issue of balance between *cognitive* (or thinking) processes, *affective* (or feeling) processes, and *interactive* (or behaving) processes. What he can do is understand better his own reaction to the learning processes offered, analysing his own behaviour as a learner, and making use of that behaviour or learning style to learn more effectively in future.

Methods of teaching and learning

Course tutors might well argue that it is very difficult to cope with the different learning styles of managers on one course. In general, the point is either ignored or dealt with by providing a variety of methods within a course, so that those who do not like one method are given a different method for another subject. There are a few cases where academics have experimented with a resource centre approach, in which course members can choose a book, a lecture, a film, or a discussion group dealing with the same subject. Such attempts have had mixed success and failure, presumably in part because managers do not experience at work the kind of leaderless, consultative democracy involved in this approach.

I hope that one of the developments in management learning will be increased attention to the need to cope with individual learning styles, so that, for example, a course on decision making could be offered in different versions to suit different styles of learning. For the moment, however, the learning manager is likely to be faced with courses which are either largely dominated by one method (such as the case study or interactive exercises), or which offer a variety of methods supposedly related to the objective of what is being taught. From the point of view of the learning manager, the important question is not how the choice of method fits an academic learning model (which is what course brochures often tell you) but how the method relates to his preferred learning style and how he will respond to it. The point could be a negative one, of avoiding certain courses dominated by one method, or a positive one, of selecting a course because of the method or methods it offers. Since most course organizers do not think much about individual learning styles, brochures give little information on which a choice could be based. I repeat my earlier advice, to talk to course organizers. The following illustrations may help to show the differences:

Case method—likely to be found most acceptable by managers who are effective leaders, good at analysis, and confident in small group discussion, probably reflective observers.

Role playing—likely to be suitable for reflective observers or experimenters, for different reasons.

Interactive skill exercises—likely to be found useful by observers and experimenters, but not by conceptualizers or concrete experiencers.

Lectures—likely to be unacceptable to many managers for different reasons; this approach does not match any style.

Business games—likely to be popular with concrete experiencers, and with reflective observers if they are not obliged to participate.

Learning styles of teachers and learners

The great problem with courses is that they are normally structured in a form seen as comfortable and appropriate by those who teach, rather than in the form which could be most appropriate for those who need to learn. A lack of congruence arises not simply because the staff are insufficiently oriented to the needs of the learners; this issue could be met by attempting to find out more about the learners and adjusting methods to suit them. The fundamental problem is that there is a lack of agreement between them on what learning is, and what style of learning is appropriate.

Two pieces of academic research illustrate the point admirably. Charles Margerison and Ralph Lewis of the Cranfield School of Management give details of research they have done which shows differences in the ways in which academics and managers approach problems, and of how they approach the problem of learning:

> Academics learn by thinking and discussing ideas on abstract levels. Managers, on the other hand, need to learn by actually doing things by trial and error. Processes that educators set up for learning reflect their own learning styles, i.e., they are basically oriented towards lectures, absorption of theoretical models, and rich in information provision such as learned papers.[1]

Hofstede[2] showed that academic faculty differed from participants on two tests of values, being more oriented to academic values such as creativity and independence of thinking and less to a will to manage, or goal orientation. The significant fact is not this unsurprising conclusion, but that the faculty rated most highly in terms of performance and response to learning those participants whose values were most similar to their own (and therefore most different from managerial norms).

It is not surprising, therefore, that those in academic institutions who are providing learning experiences often seem to participants out of tune both in terms of content and method. Since both pieces of research were carried out on managers actually attending courses, and it can reasonably be assumed that this group would tend more to academic values, the disparity between what the academic faculty provides and what many managers want is likely to be even higher. This does not mean that academic institutions are necessarily doing a bad job; they may, however, only be doing a good job with those managers whose styles match their own.

Of course, many in-company courses are not run by academics. I know of no research showing the learning styles preferred by in-company tutors. My experience has been that many of them have strong beliefs about the right learning methods, and that nowadays these beliefs most often centre on experiential learning, rather than the case method or syndicate method of ten years ago. I remember the horror with which a course tutor received the news that I proposed to start a morning on leadership styles with a twenty-minute talk on different ways of defining leadership: 'But Alan, our style is to get people to learn by doing; can't you give them some leadership exercises?'

External management education and the manager

Internal management training for managers tends to direct itself towards forms of learning that are specific to the organization; it is precisely one of their virtues when they are effective that they provide a process by which managers are socialized, to meet the particular needs of the organization for managers to behave in particular ways. Thus managers attending a general management course within an organization will, for example, learn why the particular organizational style of that organization has been determined, or will be encouraged to adopt a more participative managerial style, or will learn that the components of effective managerial behaviour in this organization include a high proportion of building on the proposals of others and a low ratio of direct disagreements.

Since I have argued consistently in this book that the needs of the manager are strongly related to his individual skills and to the particular circumstances in which he is asked to deploy those skills, it is inevitable that I approve of management training which is job specific and organization specific. Some managers will be fortunate enough to have effective internal training available to them. Others have to look outside their organization for effective course training. In the latter case, it is worth trying to define what the manager may get from attending a course; in the former case it may be helpful to describe what a manager may get from attending an external course instead of or in addition to an internal course.

Since there are a vast number of courses, with different customers, objectives, content, and standards of performance, there is a major problem in attempting to generalize. Although in doing so I will be dealing with minority provision, I have decided to concentrate on major, lengthy, business school programmes in general management, for two reasons. The first reason is that what they offer is most widely known and written about. The second reason is that they do, in fact, represent the best of what is attempted in their particular markets; for a variety of reasons, the major business schools run lengthy, ambitious programmes, generally in advantageous environments, for good quality managers. If they are doing the wrong thing—as Mant,[3] Revans, and others might argue—they are more likely to be doing it well than smaller less prestigious institutions.

What these business school general management programmes offer seems to me to differ only marginally (although the margin can be quite important). Whether it is Harvard, MIT, Stanford, Insead, the London Business School, general management programmes offer, and organizations and managers seek:

- Increased knowledge of management functions outside that of, e.g., a marketing or manufacturing manager
- An improved understanding of the business system and the processes of management
- The improvement of personal skills—particularly collecting data, analysing problems, sustaining reasoned debate, learning to learn

- The acquisition of personal insight into a manager's individual method of thinking and behaving
- The opportunity to think about himself in relation to his job
- The opportunity to breathe more deeply, think ahead in both personal and business terms
- The opportunity to learn from the experiences of others (both peers and faculty) of different approaches to familiar problems
- The opportunity to experiment in a relatively risk-free environment.

I will be turning in a later section to the issue of what those who attend courses actually get from them. For the moment, I have summarized what makes an external course a potentially fruitful learning experience.

These views are mine, drawn from discussions with course attenders, sponsors, and business school faculty. Professor R. J. Ball of the London Business School gave his views on what his institution was trying to provide, shortly after taking over as principal.[4] He thought the job of the school was to help an individual in his approach, his method, and his attitudes, but not much to help him with solutions to his day-to-day problems, His help was 'more oriented towards longer-term development of the individual, and more concerned with the general rather than the specific'. He saw one of the prime tasks to be concerned 'to build onto the personal qualities of the individual in order that he may both utilize his personal qualities more effectively and learn more rapidly from the experience he enjoys'. Information transfer was no longer the dominant element in the relationship between faculty and course members.

Professor Ball then went on to raise questions about the role of the faculty member, and the kind of help being offered, which I will deal with in my next chapter when I take up the wider issue of the various kinds of help available to the learning manager.

A slightly different view is given by Rapoport in one of the very few studies of what senior managers think of a major external course. In his view, from discussions with sponsors and the institution he studied:

> It is seen as important to give managers a break at a critical point from their ongoing pressures of career, when they are ready to pause and integrate the personal and professional significance of their life experiences so far.[5]

He thought that this kind of 'role disengagement' was an important part of the process necessary for 'role transition' (i.e., the move from specialist to generalist management). In these and other comments about the institution in which his research was conducted, Rapoport seems to me to bring out (not necessarily consciously) the particular kind of learning experience offered by a particular institution (Henley) at a particular point in time (late 'sixties).

From the learning manager's point of view, the problem with the kind of statements made by Ball and Rapoport is that they lack the specificity which would help a manager decide whether the kind of experience they are describing is likely to be an experience related to their needs as they understand them.

The learning manager is, however more likely to see the course brochure, which may tell him that 15 per cent of the course timetable is occupied by decision analysis, or that 20 per cent of the course time is concerned with the internal environment. A comparison of these different kinds of statement seems to me to reveal significant problems. What is the learning manager supposed to take away from his experience on a major post-experience programme—information, or personal development, or both? There is, indeed a dilemma expressed by House:[6] the more a management course is technique oriented and specific, the more likely it is to be obsolete—but students value techniques and specific illustrations. Interestingly, House argues in favour of problem solving and intellectual skills; he is less convinced by so-called 'principles of management', which he regards as provisional and changing. Margerison[7] argues for a radical change in the relationship between the learning manager and educators; he says that what should be present is not a transfer of knowledge and skill focused through a teacher/taught relationship, but a mutual working at the manager's problems. In his view, too frequently the manager has to make without help the transfer between what he has learned and his own situation.

Margerison's view is clearly different from that of Ball. So the learning manager would have every reason to feel confused about what he is actually going to get from a high-level management education programme. The only practical advice is to repeat what I have said earlier: the self-directed learner will take little on trust and will do what he can to find out for himself what the nature of the experience is likely to be.

Before I turn to the vital point contained in Margerison's comment—the problem of transfer of learning, of what happens when the manager re-enters his normal environment—a few comments on a special variety of learning manager.

Business graduates as managers

Business schools represent only a small proportion of the total management education and training effort. Business graduates, taking a full-time one- or two-year course in mangement, are in turn only a percentage of the business school effort. The time they spend formally learning to be managers, however, justifies a special mention.

The British experience is in numbers far behind that of the United States; in 1978, the London Business School had achieved a total output over 13 years equivalent to that achieved in that year at Harvard (just over 700). Arguments, therefore, about whether business graduates make effective managers are based on slim evidence as far as the UK is concerned. Nor is there universal agreement in the US despite the large numbers there (Livingston[8]). Any manager thinking of taking an MBA or equivalent course should surely engage in a rigorous analysis of his experience, his skills, his current organization and what an MBA course would offer, yet I have met managers who have taken such a programme with little more analysis than a general feeling that it is the kind of thing bright young managers do.

One significant benefit available to potential business graduates is that they can at least acquire more knowledge about the kind of questions to ask about the learning experience, by reading a book by a Harvard MBA.[9] It is a highly personal statement, but it is very revealing of learning processes in a way which would benefit not just potential MBAs, but any manager who is thinking of attending a major business school programme.

Problems of re-entry and transfer

The virtues of a course as a specialized learning event create problems, one of which is transferring what is learned to a normal management life.

The circumstances in which a manager who has attended a course fails to apply anything from it are well known. He may have learned nothing, because of his own lack of motivation, or because of methods of teaching inappropriate to his needs. He may have acquired knowledge or skills which are effective during the course, but which he forgets on return. There may be too big a gap between what he has learned and his working reality, so he may not have the opportunity to apply what he has learned. He may be discouraged from applying what he has learned by failings in the environment to which he has returned—the re-entry problem.

Clearly, the self-directed learner who has gone through the processes advocated in this book is likely to have fewer problems because he is more likely to have attended a course which is relevant to needs he has identified for himself, and is less likely to have learned things which are inappropriate for the environment in which he actually works (as distinct from an environment which course tutors think ought to exist). If he has also undertaken the kind of dialogue with those organizing the course which I have described earlier in this chapter, he will have clarified his expectations of it, will be more committed to the course, and be less likely to fail to get from it relevant experiences which he could transfer.

In fact, many of the problems associated with the transfer of learning and re-entry are related to what Stuart[10] has described as 'the learning contract'—the network of expectations of a course by the manager, his sponsor (employer), and the course tutors. I want to add the idea of the contract the manager signs with himself—those expectations which he may not reveal either to his employer or to the course tutors.

While, therefore, in my view many of the problems of transfer and re-entry can be resolved in advance, not all managers will have done so, and there are problems which will only be fully understood during the course. Like many other course runners, I have used the final stages of courses as a preparation for the managers' return to their normal environment by asking them to prepare action plans to take further what they have learned. While this is useful in itself as part of the learning process, and does in some cases lead to subsequent action, the only part of the transfer problem it tackles is the identification of the desirable continuity of learning. Ian McGivering of Bradford Management Centre improves this approach by using a method of tackling the re-entry issues as such. He asks course members to analyse the environment to which they will be returning and the influences on their role. When the course members have looked at the ways they are influenced by, for example, boss, subordinates colleagues and customers, they can be asked to identify what will help or hinder them in trying to make the changes identified in their action plans.

Once again, the self-directed learner will not be the victim of inaction by course organizers on this; if they do not provide the time or specific encouragement, the self-directed learner will create his own opportunities to analyse his own situation, and to discuss it with colleagues on the course.

It is characteristic of traditional approaches to training that nearly all the time on courses is devoted to acquiring information and skills, and very little to the problems the manager will have in applying them. A brief session for the production of action plans, before the final session in which course organizers receive feedback about the course, is too often all that is offered.

The kind of euphoria generated on effective courses is not always followed by effective action, because revelations and good intentions are not tested by serious consideration of the constraints on applying what has been learned. The atmosphere at the end of a successful course is rather like Shaw's description of the marriage ceremony. When people are under the influence of the most violent, most insane, most delusive, and most transient of passions, they are required to solemnly swear to remain in that excited, abnormal, and exhausting condition continuously, until death do them part.

Whatever the preparation before or during the course, problems of actually applying what has been learned will occur. Some of the problems are insoluble—for example, if what has been learned is inappropriate or unacceptable. The learning manager can, however, assist himself in applying the realistic and relevant parts of what he has learned by discussing them with his boss, colleagues, and subordinates. All too frequently, this discussion is hurried and embarrassed, and can be counterproductive if the manager seems to have become a salesman for a particular technique or message. Part of his preparation at the end of a course ought, therefore, to be to work out what he will say and to whom about what he has learned, and—perhaps most important—which allies he may be able to enlist in actually applying what he has learned. The process of monitoring and giving feedback described in the previous chapter is an important part of the action necessary for transferring improved skills or changed behaviour from the classroom to the office. Unless the learning manager provides himself with monitoring, support, and reinforcement, what he has learned will wither from lack of sustenance because most environments are unfriendly to learning and changed behaviour.

Learning from each other

It is not uncommon for managers to say that they learned more from discussions with fellow course members outside the formal sessions. This may be for some a defence mechanism to conceal either how little or how much they learned during the formal sessions, but the general principle of learning from others in a way which is in a sense distinct from the organized processes is entirely right. Most managers will have no difficulty in engaging in the kind of casual discussion about practices and ideas which is a normal feature in the nooks and crannies of a course. 'What do you do about . . .?' is a frequent and useful question. Thus some opportunities to acquire information and thereby to learn are quite well used.

Other opportunities for learning from fellow course members are not so well used. Courses offer a version of managerial behaviour which can be studied, analysed, assessed in the ways I suggested in the previous chapter. These processes can be the main feature of the course, if it is about interpersonal behaviour, but I am thinking of the opportunities which occur in courses not explicitly concerned with interpersonal skills. The problems of analysing the behaviour of others with whom you are interacting managerially are much less crucial in an environment dedicated to learning, where time spent on observing others does not involve risks on how you are perceived as a manager.

Learning is more than observing; again, courses give opportunities for exchange of information results from observation without many of the risks that arise when this is done in normal managerial work.

Do managers learn from courses?

From what I have said so far in this chapter, and indeed in the book as a whole, it should be clear that there is no general answer to this question. The obstacles in the way of effective learning are considerable, and remind me of those heavily defended beaches during the war; if you got past the mines at sea, the concrete and steel structures on the beaches, and the enfilading guns, then you might have the pleasure of meeting a German armed with a submachine gun.

Obstacles to effective learning on courses include:

- Lack of commitment on the part of the learner to the needs the course is intended to satisfy
- Lack of belief in a course, or this course, as a means of meeting needs
- Lack of credibility on the part of those running the course
- Disbelief in the possibility of changing performance after the course
- Lack of congruence between preferred learning style and the form of learning offered on the course
- Lack of contact between course content and the manager's reality.

It is a formidable list. It is still possible for some learning to occur even though one or more of the obstacles is present, but the list explains why courses often fail to meet their apparent potential in providing effective learning. Yet, although the desirable characteristics for effective learning through courses are not always present, courses continue to exist and to provide a number of trainers and educators with a pleasant living. It is possible to argue that courses exist because of the defects of other forms of learning, or because of achieved reputation rather than achieved performance. The self-directed learner, wanting to make his own decisions, wants hard evidence rather than general principle or reputation. He wants to know what the course will do for him, rather than to follow the traditions of his organization in either using or not using courses.

In fact, the self-directed learner wants to have answered an unanswerable question: 'What is the likelihood of a particular individual (me) learning the following specific things, related directly to important needs on a particular course?' One of the embarrassing things he can ask a course organizer is what data he has on desirable changes in managerial behaviour following the course. Evaluation of training effectiveness is a complex process in relation to managers, which is part of the reason why the question is embarrassing to raise; the other part is that the question is so fundamental that it is disturbing for a course organizer to be forced to reveal that there is no answer to it.

Although it is not possible to answer here a question as specific as the one with which I started the last paragraph, it is possible to give an answer at least to those who might be inclined to argue that courses are largely useless and that there is no proof that any manager's performance is significantly affected by going on a course. Even managers otherwise interested in the possibility of learning can be found in the category of agnostics, if not of atheists, in relation to the effectiveness of courses.

I will give two examples of evaluation, partly to demonstrate that there is some proof, and partly to give the self-directed learner a basis from which to ask difficult questions of course organizers

My first example is taken from a managerial skill course with which I was associated. In response to a questionnaire asking them to assess their post-course behaviour on items with which the course was concerned:

76 per cent reported that the course had helped them to control their behaviour to increase group effectiveness.

68 per cent were helped to define terms of reference and set objectives for a group task

63 per cent said the course had helped them to recognize whether the group to which they belong is working effectively on its task.

In relation to other specific behaviours, 48 per cent claim significant and lasting behaviour change on 'building' (i.e., adding to someone else's suggestion).

My second example is taken from a report by Hogarth on what managers felt had been achieved on a series of business school programmes run for a group of companies.[11] Managers who attended replied:

'Has enabled me to acquire knowledge about subjects I previously knew nothing about' (85 per cent).

Compared with an equivalent group who had not attended the programme, those who attended were found to be asking more penetrating questions, being more coherent in their reasoning, and less dominated by their functional view in defining the problems involved in a case. Managers reported themselves as considering more factors before making a decision, standing up for their ideas more, delegating more responsibility to subordinates.

Clearly, the evidence of improvement offered by these cases has to be viewed cautiously because it involves self-reporting; attempts to incorporate the views of boss or colleagues are, however, infrequent and difficult to validate. The two cases seem to me to illustrate usefully three general points for the learning manager:

- You need clear objectives before you can measure achievement
- The more course organizers retreat into generalizations about personal growth and development, the more difficult it is to evaluate learning
- Generalized measurement of achievement may not be a relevant statement for an individual; an individual's learning goals may be different from those the majority of a course wish to achieve (he may need to build more, they may need to suggest more).

I hope my general conclusion is not found to be paradoxical; it is that general evaluation of course effectiveness is desirable, but an individual's own assessment against his own goals is more meaningful. General evaluations are useful to the individual as a commentary on the professionalism of the course organizer, but may not tell the individual manager much about what he may acquire. The responsibility is back on the self-directed learner to define his own learning goals and then evaluate his own performance against them.

Questions

1. Look back at a course you have attended; would it have helped you to learn if you had known more in advance about the way in which you would be expected to learn?
2. Can you identify a relationship between your preferred style of learning and what you learned on a course you have attended? What could you do to increase your learning if you attended a similar course in future?
3. What factors influencing the way you do your job would help or hinder you if you returned from a course with new ideas for the behaviour of yourself or other people?

References

1. Margerison, C. and R. Lewis, 'Management educators and their clients'. In *Advances in Management Education*, J. Beck and T. Cox (eds) Wiley, in press.
2. Hofstede, G., 'Businessmen and business school faculty', *Journal of Management Studies*, **15**, No. 1, 1978.
3. Mant, A., *The Experienced Manager*, British Institute of Management, 1970.
4. Ball, R. J., 'The contribution of a business school to management education', *Personnel Review*, **3**, No. 1, 1974.
5. Rapoport, R. N., *Mid Career Development*, Tavistock, 1970.
6. House, R. J., 'The quest for relevance in management education', *Academy of Management Journal*, **18**, No. 2, 1975.
7. Margerison, C. J., 'Action research and action learning in management education', *Journal of European Industrial Training*, **2**, No. 6, 1978.
8. Livingston, J. S., 'Myth of the well educated manager', *Harvard Business Review*, January, 1971.
9. Cohen, P., *The Gospel According to the Harvard Business School*, Penguin, 1974.
10. Stuart, R., 'Contracting to learn', *Management Education and Development*, **9**, Part 2, 1978.
11. Hogarth, R. M., *Assessing Management Education*, MCB Publications, 1978.

10. On being helped

The need for help

I have given most weight in this book to ways in which the manager can help himself, instead of being client, patient, or victim. I have given a great deal of emphasis to the necessity for the self-directed learner to rely on his own efforts in identifying learning needs and opportunities rather than relying on the efforts of others in the organization in which he works. Yet I have also referred to the possibilities available to the manager for sharing needs, opportunities, and solutions with (particularly) his colleagues. There seems to me to be no contradiction involved in this; the distinction is between recognition and acceptance of responsibility, and making use of others in carrying out the responsibility. As Ben Jonson put it, 'Very few are wise by their own counsel or learned by their own teaching. For he that was only taught by himself had a fool for his master.' In this chapter I want to show how a manager may be helped by people other than his boss and colleagues.

The capacity to be helped

While there are a number of books and articles which tell consultants and advisers how to be effective as helpers, there is very little that I can find which advises managers on what is required of them in order that they can be effectively helped. Once more, as far as learning is concerned, the picture is familiar; the actions of those who are in business to help managers learn are given more attention than the reactions of those who are being helped to learn.

It seems to me quite crucial that a manager who is interested in learning to be effective should acquire knowledge about what is involved, in his individual case, in seeking or accepting help. There are three elements in this knowledge. He needs first of all to have his own definition of what help is, because that determines the help he should seek or accept. Second, he needs to understand those characteristics of his personal make-up which influence his attitude to help. Finally, he needs to be aware of and be able to practise those behaviours which are appropriate to seeking and receiving help.

My own efforts to give appropriate help have been assisted in recent years by remembering the story of the boy scout who gave artificial respiration to a boy who had fallen into a pond: 'I tried to give him artificial respiration, but he kept getting up and saying he wanted to change his clothes.' In my view, the most useful way of defining help is to concentrate on results rather than intentions, and to see what is offered from the point of view of the learner rather than from the point of view of the person who is offering what he, the person making the offer, considers to be help. This is not a staggeringly unrealistic view when we consider common experiences in which what is intended as help is rejected—the child who does not want to be 'helped' in playing with a toy, the adult who sees an offer of 'Let me help you by showing you how to do that' as meaning in fact 'Let me show you how much more effective I am'. Each manager has his own definition of what help is, for him. Potential helpers may, unfortunately, neither hear him asking for the help he wants, nor hear him rejecting the help he does not want. Thus, a manager could reject help from an adviser couched in terms of analysing his learning needs, but could accept help from the same adviser on analysing how he spends his time.

Of course, there are problems unresolved by saying that help is what the recipient perceives as help, not what the man offering help intends. A learner may ask for help in a form which will not, in fact, be helpful. For example, one manager with whom I was involved was very keen for me to show him directly how to carry out a particular task; my view as his adviser was that offering that kind of help would be temporarily popular but ineffective in the long term. I therefore tried to balance giving what he saw as help with what I believed to be a more important form of help, which was to get him to look at the problem instead of modelling his behaviour on me. A manager may often recognize and want help to alleviate symptoms, rather than recognizing and attempting to deal with causes.

However, only by facing such paradoxes will the learning manager really be able to define and work from his underlying attitude to help. I do not pretend that it is either an easy or a popular task; it is perhaps too elusive, too much dependent on reflective modes of thought.

I have fewer inhibitions about suggesting that managers should look at those aspects of their personal make-up which may influence them in seeking or receiving help. In many respects, the characteristics of effective learners described in chapter 5 have a strong relationship with the characteristics of managers who are able to accept help. For example, a manager whose learning style is dominated by modelling is less likely to be interested in help than someone whose style is based on experimentation. The characteristics of someone likely to be able to ask for or receive help seem to me to be these:

- A self-image which would not be damaged by help
- An optimistic rather than a pessimistic view of the possibility of personal improvement
- An openness to new data, even where this conflicts with old data which may be more acceptable to the manager
- A secure feeling of basic personal effectiveness, or alternatively a high degree of concern about basic personal effectiveness; one person may be

secure and therefore not see help as a criticism. Another person may be insecure but accept help because he is desperate

- An ability to accept a degree of dependency on someone else, and a degree of vulnerability to him.

I have no inhibitions at all about suggesting the behaviours appropriate for a manager who is interested in receiving help on learning. A manager who might be uncomfortable with the kind of self-analysis involved in the first two elements in the capacity to be helped is not so likely to find it difficult to accept and implement ideas about specific forms of behaviour. Here are some kinds of behaviour which he needs to show in order to get acceptable and useful help on learning:

- Discussing the standards which could be appropriate for one or more aspects of his management performance
- Positively showing a wish to be helped by seeking specific information ('Should I start the meeting by asking for agreement on the agenda?')
- Asking for information which may be uncomfortable rather than warming ('Why did things go wrong from the start of the meeting?')
- Accepting information as neutral data rather than implied criticism deserving disagreement ('You say I interrupt other people too frequently; can you tell me more about how the interruptions look to you?')
- Monitoring the number of encouraging responses he makes to information intended to help, and the number of defensive responses
- Rewarding the person who is giving help not only by expressing gratitude but by showing him that what you do has been affected by the help he gave.

This last point is especially important. In learning terms, a rewarding behaviour tends to cause repetition; rewarding someone who has given effective help means that he is likely to repeat the behaviour which he has learned is acceptable. This means more help from him, and indeed may mean that he experiments with additional forms of help. Conversely, the absence of reward tends to reduce the occasions on which help is offered. Reward is absolutely crucial because well intentioned help goes wrong so often that people become far too conservative both in asking for and offering help, because of uncertainty. Reward to the help decreases uncertainty.

In total, the behaviour required from the learner who wishes to be helped is that collection of behaviours which will enable others to take the risks and seize the opportunies of helping him effectively. The constraints and inhibitions which prevent him from behaving in this way are part of the fearful ineffectiveness of much of our managerial behaviour. A demonstration of these inhibitions can be seen in the adventurous behaviour sometimes adopted by managers in 'stranger' groups, where they feel uninhibited by organizational expectations. In the wider world, they can be seen in the tasks carried out by people under hypnosis, tasks which in their conscious mind they would believe to be impossible. Managers are constrained in their behaviour by beliefs about what is and is not acceptable in their organizational environment; asking for help on really important learning issues means overcoming the constraints implying that such a behaviour is something the successful effective manager does not indulge in.

Understanding the need to learn

While I have generalized about the capacity to be helped, help clearly comes in different forms at different stages of the learning process and at different levels of awareness of what help is. Chapter 3 gave most weight to ways in which the individual manager could analyse his own learning needs, rather than relying on general analyses of needs of groups of managers. General analyses can, however, be an appropriate part of a total approach to identifying needs; they provide a general base against which the individual manager can assess his individual needs. The most detailed study of individual manager development, carried out in the American company AT&T,[1] shows the kind of stimulus to identifying learning needs which a general analysis can provide. This study covers the early years of 247 college graduates, and among other things looked at some managerial skills measured through tests in an assessment centre. In general, over eight years, there was no improvement in skills of organizing, planning, and decision making, while scores in general on behaviour flexibility, oral communication, and likeableness actually went down. The startling general finding was that there was no change in overall management ability for the average recruit. In a company likely to be no worse than others in the kind of learning experiences it provided, the results gave no support for the notion that experience is the best teacher. While, of course, some individuals showed improvement on some skills, it is difficult not to recognize the validity of the conclusion that there was a need for more deliberate attempts to foster such abilities.

Few organizations are equipped to provide valid evidence on learning needs in this kind of way, but the study illustrates the different perspective which can be offered by this kind of analysis. Young managers assessing themselves only against the general performance of their contemporaries can be using inappropriate standards. This analysis could be used to give them a more relevant understanding of what their needs might be.

A second illustration of the value of external help in understanding learning needs is seen in Warner Burke,[2] who I have quoted earlier in this book in relation to the special learning needs of women. What Burke has to say could be illuminating to women managers, in helping them to understand themselves and their environment better; it could also be helpful to male managers by helping them to identify and then modify their reactions to women in

177

management. Burke says that men tend to place women in one of four stereo-typed roles:

—Mother
—Seductress
—Pet
—Iron maiden

Women managers need to learn how to get away from this stereotyping, male managers need to learn how to avoid awarding the stereotypes. These learning requirements will arise, increasingly, not mainly from any ethical issues of equality or justice, but from the practical fact that there are going to be more women managers. The male majority needs help first in recognizing their learning needs in relation to female subordinates, colleagues, or superiors. Outside help is crucial in assisting even the most self-analytical learner recognize his needs in areas of deep conditioning such as this.

Aspects of relationships such as these are, of course, productive not only of objective learning needs but of emotional disturbance to a level which can become real stress. Outside help may be the only way of causing managers to recognize stress, and of identifying ways of learning to cope with it if it cannot be eliminated.

The kind of help identified above is relatively unchallenging; managers would be taking few risks in exposing themselves to these impersonal forms of stimulus.

Chapter 3 referred briefly to methods of analysing managerial learning needs by an adviser looking at the needs of groups of managers; such analyses can stimulate the individual manager to understand his own needs better, as well as providing data for general statements about needs for managers—for example, in identifying that all general managers need to know more about assessing competitor competencies. Questionnaires introduced or developed by an adviser which cause a manager to look at his needs in detail, as illustrated by Pedler *et al.*,[3] can also be helpful.

While, therefore, I have largely concentrated in this book on things which a manager can do without professional help, the illustrations I have now given should show that suggestions from others about types of need can be useful. For most managers, however, this kind of stimulus is likely to be peripheral and relatively uninfluential. The really influential help is that given directly on an individual basis.

Help with the learning process

There has been a major gap in the kind of non-managerial help available to a manager who has some recognition of his need to learn. At one extreme have been management development advisers, equipped with knowledge about general systems for identifying learning needs such as appraisal or training needs analysis, or knowledgeable about methods and resources such as the

Harvard Advanced Management Programme, or familiar with the difference between action learning and action training. At the other extreme have been management trainers and management educators, bristling with knowledge of particular subjects and sometimes also expert in ways of conveying the knowledge. In more recent years, these occupations have been joined by advisers on organizational development, a large part of whose expertise has focused on issues of how individuals or units relate to each other in interpersonal terms, and how people can learn to manage the present situation better or learn to manage the change to a new situation.

Many managers would have a problem in understanding the difference between management developers, management trainers, and organization developers. My purpose here is not to explain and justify the distinction between these functions, but to assist a manager to understand better what he is being offered, so that he can both make more effective use of the help he is being offered and also look for a different kind of help if the offer is not sufficient for his needs.

The first point to recognize is that most of these advisers are constrained by economic factors to give a service focused on general rather than specific needs; they are unlikely to be geared to providing the individual manager with help which is directly related to his needs, because of the time and effort necessary to establish what those needs are. It is expensive for an adviser to work with an individual on his learning needs, instead of working on an improved appraisal scheme for 400 managers. It is expensive for a tutor to give specific coaching to an individual manager on his interviewing skills, instead of running a two-day course for eight managers.

There are other reasons than economics why advice is geared to general rather than specific needs, of which the most important is the interaction of the stereotypes held by the manager of the kind of help he expects, and the stereotypes held by advisers and trainers of the help they are expected to provide. This interaction leads to a self-selection situation, in which people capable of providing a particular kind of service occupy those roles, and little is done either to challenge the roles or to improve the competence of the people in them.

Looking for help within the company

Managers are in a powerful position to improve the kind of help they receive on learning from specialist advisers within the company. The kind of service most frequently provided is concerned with overall schemes, setting up large-scale processes for reviewing needs, assessing performance. Managers have the power to ask for the kind of alternative service which deals with individual needs. The learning manager should be able to recognize and seek for help for himself as an individual, using the knowledge of the kind of help he might benefit from by testing the various stages of the learning process set out in this book. He would then be less likely to be satisfied at the low-risk help on large-scale processes of manager development. The learning manager would behave in some of the following ways:

Instead of asking for	*He would ask for*
A new appraisal form	Comments on appraisal he had completed
A good general management course	An appraisal of his learning needs
A course on chairmanship	Observation and comments on a meeting he chaired
A book on decision making	An analysis of the decisions he made over five days
Recommendations on the latest manager development technique	An assessment of his learning style in comparison with that implied by the technique
A review of manager skills	Help with analysis of what he actually does
The importation of managerial grid, or System 4, or Theory X	Discussion of methods of assessing his management style

Unfortunately, he might not immediately have available to him advisers who can give him the kind of help he wants. This is why I make the point that the manager is in a powerful position to secure the kind of help he wants, because he can press for a different kind of adviser or ask for additional help within the company or secure in special help from outside. He may want, for example, the kind of direct assistance on learning in which his helper sits with him and bases his help on observation of his managerial behaviour, the kind of help described by Hague,[4] Honey,[5] and Mumford[6]—a powerful if luxurious learning aid. He is unlikely to get this from management development advisers and trainers whose skill and experience, and the help they can offer, is geared to the quite different expectations illustrated by the left-hand column, and to the rewards which organizations give for being able to carry out those activities.

The kind of illustrations I have given of the real help on the learning process which ought to be available to the manager could help managers to secure a better service, even though they may make the lives of management development advisers and trainers more uncomfortable.

I have concentrated on the role of the adviser in-company because, as chapter 9 pointed out, courses give insufficient attention to helping managers to understand the learning process in which they are involved, and too little is done to help managers with the problem of transferring knowledge from a course to real life. As I showed in that chapter, more help can be sought from tutors than the formal timetable seems to allow.

Learning for life

There is no necessary reason why managers should stop learning as they get older; they learn less because they are not willing to take the risks involved in recognizing and dealing with their needs. Equally, although the focus of this book has been on helping a manager meet the demands for effective performance in his organization, the principles and many of the practices can be applied to make a more effective life outside work. But the details of how to do this require another book.

Questions

1. Look back over your experiences of advisers trying to help you learn; what has your reaction been?
2. Which forms of help have you found acceptable?
3. How do your reactions to attempts to help you compare with the suggested types of behaviour on page 176?

References

1. Bray, D. W., R. J. Campbell and D. L. Grant, (eds), *Formative Years in Business*, Krieger, 1974.
2. Warner Burke, W., in *Current Issues in Organization Development*, Human Sciences Press, 1977.
3. Pedler, M., J. Burgoyne and T. Boydell, *A Manager's Guide to Self Development*, McGraw-Hill, 1978.
4. Hague, H., 'The action teaching catalyst', *Management Today*, November 1977.
5. Honey, P., 'On the trail of the personnel professional', *Personnel Management*, April 1976.
6. Mumford, A. C., 'Management development and the powers of observation', *Personnel Management*, October 1976.

Index

183

Printed in Great Britain
by W & J Mackay Limited, Chatham